PagePlus X6
Resource Guide

Contacting Serif

Contacting Serif technical support

Our support mission is to provide fast, friendly technical advice and support from a team of on-call experts. Technical support is provided from our web support page, and useful information can be obtained via our web-based forums (see below).

UK/International/
US Technical Support: http://www.support.serif.com/

Additional Serif contact information

Web:

Serif website:	http://www.serif.com
Forums:	http://www.serif.com/forums.asp

Main office (UK, Europe):

The Software Centre, PO Box 2000, Nottingham, NG11 7GW, UK

Main:	(0115) 914 2000
Registration (UK only):	(0800) 376 1989
Sales (UK only):	(0800) 376 7070
Customer Service (UK/International):	http://www.support.serif.com/
General Fax:	(0115) 914 2020

North American office (US, Canada):

Serif Inc, The Software Center, 4041 MacArthur Blvd., Suite 120, Newport Beach, CA 92660, USA

Registration:	(800) 794-6876
Sales:	(800) 489-6703
Customer Service:	(800) 489-6720

International enquiries

Please contact our main office.

Credits

This Resource Guide, and the software described in it, is furnished under an end user License Agreement, which is included with the product. The agreement specifies the permitted and prohibited uses.

Trademarks

Copyrights

Introduction

Welcome to the PagePlus X6 **Resource Guide! Wh**ether you are new to
PagePlus or a seasoned desktop publisher, this guide offers content to
help you get the best out of PagePlus.

From a range of illustrated tutorials to get you started or help you
accomplish a complex project, to full-colour previews of the theme
layouts and Pro Template Packs, we hope you'll find this Resource Guide
to be a valuable resource that you'll return to time and time again.

The Resource Guide is organized into the following chapters:

1: Tutorials

Illustrated, step-by-step training covering the basics of PagePlus and
desktop publishing.

2: Theme Layouts

Full-colour page previews of the theme layout sets included with
PagePlus X6.

3: Pro Template Packs

A reference gallery of the Pro Template Packs included with PagePlus X6.

Contents

Tutorials

Whether you are new to **Serif PagePlus X6** or an experienced user, these tutorials will help you to get the best out of the program.

From beginner-level to advanced, these tutorials will help you to learn how to use the fundamental PagePlus tools. We'll have you producing great desktop publications, regardless of your current skill level!

Accessing the tutorials

You can access the tutorials in one of the following ways:

- From the PagePlus X6 Startup Wizard, select from the **Learn** section. Different icons indicate the type of tutorial available.

 a video tutorial

 an online tutorial

 see more tutorials and videos!

- or -

- From PagePlus, click **Help** and then click **Tutorials**.

Accessing the sample files

Throughout the tutorials, you'll be prompted to access sample files. All samples are accessible via the Internet at the following location:

http://go.serif.com/resources/PPX6

If you've clicked on a file, you can either open or save the file. We recommend you save the file to your desktop or a named folder on your computer.

Useful icons

Before we get started, here is a quick guide to the icons that you'll find useful along the way.

When you see this icon, there are project files and/or images available for download that will help you to complete the tutorial. Sometimes we provide you with partially completed projects so that you can concentrate on the main learning point of the tutorial, without having to recreate our design.

Don't forget to save your work! It's good practice to save often. We'll remind you along the way with these helpful save points.

This is a note. Notes provide useful information about the program or a particular technique.

This is a tip. Our tips provide information that will help you with your projects.

This is a warning! We don't want to make you panic but when you see this icon, you need to pay attention to the steps as they will be particularly important.

Exploring PagePlus X6

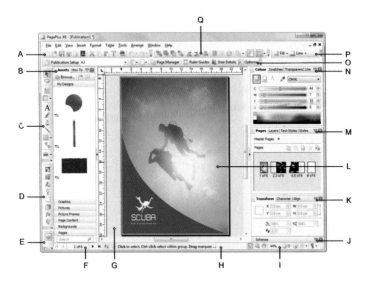

(A) Standard toolbar, (B) Assets & How To tab, (C) Tools toolbar, (D) Attributes toolbar, (E) Studio toolbar, (F) Page Navigation toolbar, (G) Pasteboard, (H) Hintline toolbar, (I) View tools, (J) Schemes tab (collapsed), (K) Transform, Character & Align tabs, (L) Page area, (M) Pages, Layers, Text Styles & Styles tabs, (N) Colour, Swatches, Transparency & Line tabs, (O) Context toolbar, (P) Colours toolbar, (Q) Arrange toolbar.

The PagePlus workspace

The PagePlus workspace consists of:

- Your **page** area (L), for placing text, graphics, and other objects that will appear in the final publication.

- The **pasteboard** area (G), for storing page elements before being positioned on the page area. Objects on the pasteboard are accessible from any page. (The pasteboard and any objects on it will not be appear when your document is published.)

- The **Assets** tab, for storing and enabling quick access to content such as graphics, pictures, frames, backgrounds, and page layouts.

- A range of other **tabs**, to help you organize your workflow and modify your publication design.

  ➤Tab groups can be hidden or displayed by clicking the arrows on the left and right of the workspace.

- Horizontal and vertical **toolbars**, used to access PagePlus commands and tools. Including the **Studio** toolbar, which allows you to display specific tabs and quickly show or hide all tabs.

 Move the mouse pointer around the screen and you'll see popup **tooltips** that identify toolbar buttons and flyouts.

 Right-click any object or page region to bring up a **context menu** of functions.

Frame Text

This tutorial shows how to create and manipulate frames, frame text, and use text styles.

By the end of this tutorial you will be able to:

- Select and edit text.

- Create new text frames.

- Link story text between frames.

- Format and get creative with text frames.

- Create placeholder text.

- Apply and modify text styles.

Go to **http://go.serif.com/resources/PPX6** to download the following tutorial project file(s):

 frame.ppp

Let's begin...

* On the Standard toolbar, click  **Open**.

* Locate the **frame.ppp** file and click **Open**.

  The project opens in the workspace.

 Save now! On the **File** menu click **Save As...** In the dialog, browse to the location in which you want to save the file, type in a new name and click **Save**.

About frame text

PagePlus provides two types of text—*frame text* and *artistic text*. Frame text is placed on the page inside a *text frame*, and is generally used for body copy and longer passages of text, or non-decorative text such as contact details, product information, etc.

Artistic text is most often used for titles and decorative text. For more on artistic text, see the tutorial *Artistic Text* on p. 25.

Frame text has several special properties. It enables you to:

* Flow text between linked frames.

* Wrap text around pictures and shapes.

* Shape the frame to page objects.

 Many of the methods described in the following sections, such as selecting and editing text, are applicable to both artistic and frame text.

To begin, we'll show you how to select, edit, and format text.

To select and edit text:

1. Click on the title 'Newsletter' at the top of the page. The Hintline toolbar tells you that this is a *text frame*.

2. Click to place an insertion point before the 'N' and then drag to the right to select the entire line of text.

3. Type 'DIVE LOGS'.

The title is complete and you've now used one of the methods to select text. Let's move on to look at some of the ways we can edit a text frame.

Linked frames

In PagePlus, you can link multiple text frames. This allows the text to flow from one frame to another automatically. Click inside the text frame containing the placeholder text.

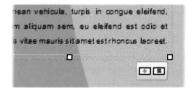

The frame shows two different buttons, AutoFlow and Overflow. These show that the frame contains more story text than can be displayed in the frame. We can fix this in several ways. To start with, we'll create a new text frame and link the story text.

To create a new text frame:

1. On the Tools toolbar, click the  Standard Text Frame.

2. Move the cursor in line with the top of the first frame. A set of column guides appear when the cursor is correctly positioned.

3. Click and drag across and down the page until the next set of column guides appear on the right, and the bottom page margin guide appears below.

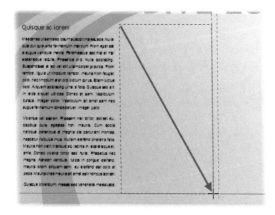

The frame is created when you release the mouse button.

Now that we have an empty frame, we can link this frame to the text frame that contains the overflow text.

To link existing text frames:

1. Click inside the text frame containing the placeholder text. The  AutoFlow and Overflow buttons are displayed.

2. Click the Overflow button. The cursor will change to .

3. Hover over the new text frame and click once when the edges glow.

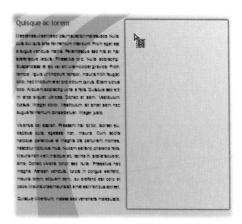

The text flows into the new frame, which is now linked to the first frame.

As you can see, the ⊞ AutoFlow and ▣ Overflow buttons are still available, meaning that the linked frames still contain additional text.

Click inside the first frame. Notice that a  Continued (Overflow) button is displayed. This indicates that the frame is now linked, but that the last frame in the sequence still contains overflow text. Let's fix this now.

To create a linked text frame:

1. Click inside the second text frame so that the AutoFlow and Overflow buttons are displayed.

2. Click the Overflow button. The cursor will change to.

3. Move the pointer in line with the top of the second frame. A set of column guides appear when the pointer is correctly positioned.

4. Click and drag across and down the page until a page margin appears on the right and another at the bottom of the page.

5.   The linked frame is created when you release the mouse button, and is filled with the overflowing story text from the previous frames.

Notice that the frame now displays a  No Overflow button, indicating that all of the story text is now displayed in a frame.

If you click in either of the first two frames, a Continued button displays indicating that the frames are linked and that the complete story text is displayed in one or more linked frames.

Don't forget to save your work!

Working with text frames

In the previous example, we created a three column layout using three linked frames. However, a single frame can have multiple columns. This can help simplify the layout design as it takes the worry out of aligning multiple frames. Let's look at this now.

To change the frame layout:

1. On the **Pages** tab, double-click on the page 2 thumbnail to display the page.

2. Click once in the text frame to select it.

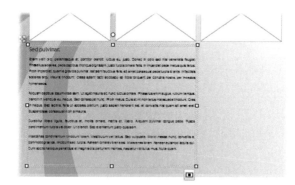

3. On the Text context toolbar, set the column number to **2**.

The text frame updates to contain 2 columns.

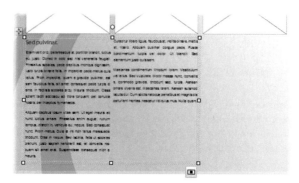

 Don't forget to save your work!

Getting creative with frames

For our next example, we'll show you how to make your frame a little more creative by adding some colour.

To create a colour-filled text frame:

1. On the Tools toolbar, click the ![icon] Standard Text Frame.

2. Move the cursor in line with the top of the first frame. A set of column guides appear when the cursor is correctly positioned.

3. Click and drag across and down the page until a page margin appears on the right and another at the bottom of the page.

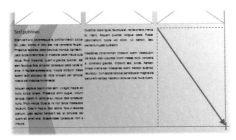

The frame is created when you release the mouse button.

4.   Select the border of the frame (it will change to a solid outline).

5.   On the Swatches tab, click the 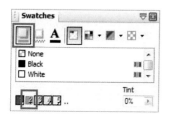 Fill button and then click the Scheme Colour 2 swatch.

The fill is applied.

To insert and format text using text styles:

1. Click inside the text frame to create an insertion point, and then type "Diving News".

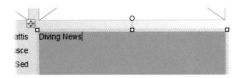

2. On the **Text Styles** tab, click the 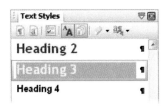 **Show All** button, and then click 'Heading 3'.

The heading style is applied.

Notice that the text is tight against the frame edge? Although this is what we want normally in a frame, as this is a coloured frame, it would look better if we added some internal padding to the frame edge.

To add frame padding:

1. On the Text context toolbar, click 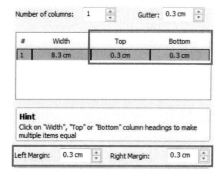 Frame Setup.

2. In the dialog:

- On column 1, set the Top and Bottom to 0.3 cm.

- Set the Left Margin to 0.3 cm.

- Set the Right Margin to 0.3 cm.

Number of columns:	1		Gutter:	0.3 cm	

#	Width	Top	Bottom
1	8.3 cm	0.3 cm	0.3 cm

Hint
Click on "Width", "Top" or "Bottom" column headings to make
multiple items equal

Left Margin:	0.3 cm		Right Margin:	0.3 cm	

- Click OK.

  The frame is updated.

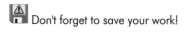 Don't forget to save your work!

Text styles

If you use styles to format text, you have the advantage that if you want to change the style, all instances of that formatting also update. Let's try this now.

To create placeholder text:

1. Click inside the text frame at the end of the word "News" and press **Enter** to drop to the next line.

2. On the **Insert** menu, click **Fill with Placeholder Text** (or press F5).

As you can see, the text is black and does not have great contrast against the coloured background. We could change this by simply selecting the text and applying a different colour. However, if we were likely to use this type of text frame again, a better approach is to create or modify a text style.

To modify a text style to change text formatting:

1. Click on the placeholder text inside the coloured text frame. On the
    Text Styles tab, you will see that the text is assigned the 'Artistic Body'
    paragraph style (and a Placeholder character style).

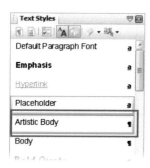

2. On the Text Styles tab, hover over the 'Artistic Body' style, click the
    drop-down arrow that displays and select **Modify Artistic Body...**
    from the menu.

3. In the Text Style dialog:

    *   Expand the **Character** category and click the **Font** sub-category.

    *   In the **Text fill:** drop-down menu, select the Scheme Colour 5
        swatch.

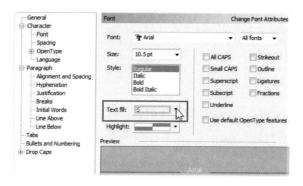

- Click **OK**.

The modified style is applied to the text.

It's also possible to update a text style to match any formatting that you've applied to the text on the page.

To update a text style:

1. On the **Pages** tab, double-click the page 1 thumbnail to display the page.

2. Triple-click anywhere on the words "DIVE LOGS". The entire line is selected.

3. On the Text context toolbar, select a different font. (We chose Xpress Heavy SF.)

4. Right-click the selected text and in the **Text Format** menu, click Update Text Style.

5. In the warning dialog, click **Yes** to confirm the update to the style in the entire document.

6. In the **Text Styles** tab, you'll see that the Heading 1 style has been updated to match the text and is available to use in your document.

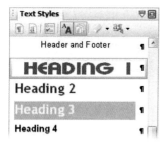

You now know how to edit and format text, create new frame text objects, and edit text frame properties.

The skills you have acquired should be sufficient for most of your PagePlus projects, but you'll find more detailed information in PagePlus Help. If you haven't done so already, why not try the tutorial *Artistic Text* on p. 25?

Artistic Text

In this tutorial, we'll show you how to create and manipulate artistic text. Artistic text is standalone text that can be typed directly onto a page. Its unique properties make it especially useful for titles, pull quotes, and other special-purpose text.

By the end of this tutorial you will be able to:

- Place and format artistic text.

- Apply a gradient fill to text.

- Apply a reflection effect style to text.

- Create shaped text (or text-on-a-path).

- Change the colour scheme.

Over the next few pages, we'll create a poster using artistic text objects. Along the way, you'll learn how to apply some of the stunning visual effects available in PagePlus.

 Go to http://go.serif.com/resources/PPX6 to download the following tutorial project file(s):

🔵 artistic.ppp

Let's begin...

- On the Standard toolbar, click  Open.

- Locate the **artistic.ppp** file and click **Open**.

   The project opens in the workspace.

Placing and formatting Artistic text

Although we are working with artistic text in this tutorial, many of the methods described below are applicable to both artistic and frame text. The special properties of artistic text allow you to:

- Stretch or squash the text to create a stylistic effect.

- Create shaped text by putting the text on a path.

Now let's create a new artistic text object...

To create artistic text:

1. On the Tools toolbar, click the **A** Artistic Text Tool.

2. Click anywhere on your page to set a text insertion point.

3. On the Text context toolbar, in the Text Styles drop-down list, select TITLE.

4. Type 'ANACONDA DESIGN'.

Now that our basic title is placed, let's make it a little more interesting.

To accurately resize and rotate artistic text:

1. With the text object still selected, on the **Transform** tab, ensure that the **Lock Aspect Ratio** is off. (If not, click the button once.)

2. Change the Width to **38.0 cm** and then change the Height to **10.0 cm**.

3. Finally, rotate the object by **5°**. (For quick rotation, use the rotation 'lollipop' handle.)

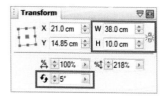

4. On the Align tab, ensure that **Relative to: Page** is selected and then click 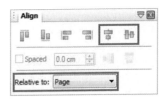 Centre Vertically and Centre Horizontally.

Using gradient fills on text

The title already has a lot more impact, but we can make it even more powerful by applying a gradient fill.

To apply a gradient fill:

1. Click the border of the text object to select it (the border turns solid) and then click on the **Swatches** tab.

2. Expand the Gradient Fills flyout and select **Linear**.

3. Click the **Linear Fill 14** swatch to apply it to the text.

The gradient colour spread works well, but we can make it fit the overall colour scheme better by changing it to use scheme colours.

To edit a gradient fill:

1. Ensure the text object is selected and then on the Attributes toolbar, click the 🔥 Fill Tool.

The object's fill path is displayed.

2.   On the Fill context toolbar:

- In the **Fill Start** drop-down list, select swatch 5 on the Scheme 5 row.

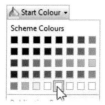

- In the **Fill End** drop-down list, select swatch 5 on the Scheme 4 row.

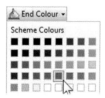

3.   (Optional) You can also adjust the fill path by clicking and dragging the fill path nodes.

Using Styles

The title is almost complete; however, let's make it look really special by adding a reflection effect.

To apply a reflection effect:

1. With the text object selected, go to the **Styles** tab and, in the categories drop-down list, select **Reflection**.

2. In the **Artistic Text Reflections** sub-category (you may need to scroll down), click the **Text Reflection 02 : FilterEffects** preset.

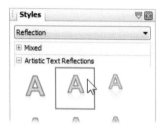

The reflection is applied.

To edit a reflection effect:

1.   With the text object selected, on the Attributes toolbar, click the
     fx Filter Effects button.

2.   Drag the dialog to the side so that you can see the text on the page.
     In the dialog:

     •   Drag the **Offset** slider to the left until the reflection sits just
         below the text.

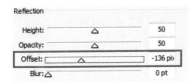

     •   Click **OK**.

         The reflection is updated.

Text on a path

For the final step, we are going to add the company website URL to the poster. For that extra special touch, we'll create it on a curved path.

To place text on a path:

1. On the Tools toolbar, click the **A** Artistic Text Tool.

2. Click anywhere on your page to create a text insertion point and on the Text context toolbar, set the font size to **48 pt**.

3. Go to the Swatches tab, click the **A** Text button and then click the Scheme Colour 4 swatch.

4. On the Insert menu, select Information > User Details...

5. In the dialog, select (Business) Web Site URL and click OK.

    The company URL stored in the User Details is inserted on the page. (Note: We updated our User Details to match this scenario.)

6. On the Text context toolbar, in the  **Path Text** drop-down list, select **Path - Wave**. The path is applied.

7. To stretch the path, drag the square Start and End nodes (yellow highlight).

 The square nodes control the length of the path, whereas the arrow handles control the start and end points of the text with respect to the path's length. For more details, see PagePlus Help.

8. To adjust the slope of the path, click on a Start or End node and then drag its curve handle (blue highlight).

9. (Optional) Resize the text object by clicking and dragging the top and side edge resize handles.

10. Finally, click and drag the ⊞ **Move** button, or the object border, to move the object into position as illustrated.

Changing the colour scheme

The poster is complete! However, we'll take this opportunity to illustrate why we used scheme colours to colour our text...

To change the colour scheme:

- On the **Schemes** tab, click to select a different scheme. (The **Schemes** tab is collapsed by default at the bottom right of the studio.) We selected **Scheme 3**.

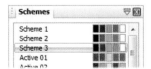

All of the schemed objects update!

This makes it easy to change the overall look and feel of your publication without any extra work. To find out more, and for help creating your own schemes, see the tutorials *Colour Schemes* (p. 125) and *Colour Schemes II: Custom Schemes* (p. 137).

We hope that you've enjoyed this tutorial. You should now be quite adept at using artistic text. If you haven't done so already, why not try the tutorial *Frame Text* on p. 7? Have fun!

Pictures

The right pictures can make your publication stand out from the crowd. PagePlus offers a variety of tools and techniques for working with the pictures within your publication.

By the end of this tutorial you will be able to:

● Add pictures to existing frames.

● Use the Assets tab.

● Insert a new frame.

● Apply image adjustments.

● Insert an inline graphic.

● Apply wrap settings to an object.

Go to http://go.serif.com/resources/PPX6 to download the following tutorial project file(s):

⊙ pictures.ppp

Let's begin...

- On the Standard toolbar, click ⬚ **Open**.

- Locate the **pictures.ppp** file and click **Open**.

  The project opens in the workspace.

- On the **Pages** tab, double-click the page 2 thumbnail to display the page in the workspace.

Adding pictures to an existing frame

This page provides two 'placeholder' picture frames. We'll now look at the different ways in which you can add pictures to the frames.

We'll be using the sample images installed with PagePlus. However, you can use your own images if you prefer.

To add a single picture to a frame:

1. Click to select the large picture frame and then click the 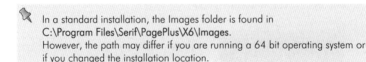 Replace Picture button. The Import Picture dialog opens.

2. In the Import Picture dialog, browse to your Images folder.

> In a standard installation, the Images folder is found in C:\Program Files\Serif\PagePlus\X6\Images.
> However, the path may differ if you are running a 64 bit operating system or if you changed the installation location.

3. Select the group diving picture (2838416.jpg) and click Open.

The picture is added to the frame and scaled to fit.

When the picture is selected, note that the picture frame toolbar displays in the lower-right corner.

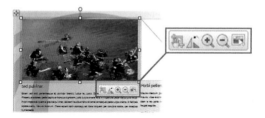

You can use these tools to adjust your picture inside the frame.

To adjust a picture inside a frame:

* To reposition the picture inside the frame, click 🖼 **Pan**, and then click and drag on the picture with the 🖑 cursor.

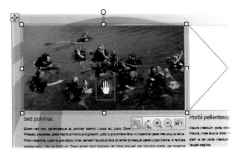

* To rotate the picture anti-clockwise, in 90° increments, click 🔄 **Rotate**.

* To zoom in or out of the picture, click 🔍 **Zoom In** or 🔍 **Zoom Out**.

* To replace the picture, click 🖼 **Replace Picture**, browse to and select a new picture, then click **Open**.

Using the Assets tab

If you're working with lots of pictures, or are not sure which of your pictures will work best in your publication, you might prefer to add them to the **Assets** tab before adding them to the layout.

PagePlus X6 is supplied with several **Asset packs** containing pictures, graphics, backgrounds and various other page elements.

For the next section of the tutorial, we'll use some of the assets found in the **Tutorials** assets pack.

To add tutorial assets to the Assets tab:

1. On the **Assets** tab, click **Browse...** to open the **Asset Browser**.

2. In the **Pack Files** section, expand the **Tutorials** folder and click to select the **Tutorials** pack.

3. To display only the pictures, press the **Ctrl** key and then click the **Pictures** category.

4. Click each of the diving related thumbnails. The green ● shows that it has been added to the tab.

5. Click **Close** to exit.

You can also add your own pictures to the **Assets** tab, and even save them as an Asset pack for use in other projects. For information on how to do this, see the **How To** tab and PagePlus Help.

Now that we have imported our pictures, we can add them to the page.

To add a picture to an existing frame:

1. On the **Assets** tab, the **Pictures** category should be displayed (if not, click the header).

2. Drag the picture of the air cylinder onto the empty picture frame. The picture is cropped to fit the frame boundary.

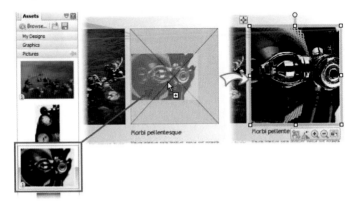

In this instance, the picture doesn't really work on the page. However, by using frames for your pictures, it's easy to replace one picture with another.

To replace a picture in a frame:

● Drag the picture of the gauges from the **Assets** tab and onto the square frame.

The picture adjusts to fit the neatly inside the frame even though it is a different size and aspect ratio.

Inserting a blank picture frame

Now that page 2 is complete, let's have a look at page 1. Along the way, we'll show you some more image techniques. First of all, on the **Pages** tab, double-click the page 1 thumbnail.

To insert a picture frame:

1. On the Tools toolbar, on the Picture flyout, click the ⊠ Rectangular Picture Frame.

2.   Position the cursor near to the text as illustrated. You should see the dynamic guides appear.

3.   Click and drag to begin creating the frame. Release the mouse button when the edges line up with the dynamic guides at the edges of the page.

4.   Drag the picture of the two divers from the **Assets** tab and onto the picture frame.

5. Click the 🔍 **Zoom In** button a couple of times to zoom into the image, then click the 🔲 **Pan** button to position the divers in the centre of the frame.

Applying image adjustments

When you select a picture, the Picture context toolbar displays at the top of the workspace, automatically.

This toolbar provides quick and easy access to key picture-related controls—replace, resize, recolour, and so on—and also lets you apply useful image adjustments, such as red eye removal and brightness and contrast adjustments, with a single click.

Advanced image adjustments
PagePlus includes a powerful mix of advanced image correction and
adjustment tools— including levels, colour balance, channel mixer, HSL, and
Unsharp Mask—and a selection of creative effects such as Diffuse Glow and
Gaussian Blur.

All of these are applied from the PhotoLab dialog, which you can open by
clicking 🔘 PhotoLab on the Picture context toolbar.

For more information, see PagePlus Help.

Adding an 'inline' object

If you are working with text and images in a publication, you can obtain
fine control over object positioning using object anchoring. We'll
introduce this by adding a small inline image to the title.

For the next section of the tutorial, we'll use some of the assets found in
the Tutorials assets pack.

To add tutorial assets to the Assets tab:

1. On the Assets tab, click 🔲 Browse... to open the Asset Browser.

2. In the Pack Files section, expand the Tutorials folder and click to
    select the Tutorials pack.

3. In the **Graphics** category, click the thumbnails of the two silhouettes.

4. Click **Close** to exit.

To add an inline image:

1. On the **Assets** tab, the **Graphics** category should be displayed (if not, click the header).

2. Drag the silhouette of the shark onto the page.

3. Resize the silhouette so that it fits the size of the text. If you haven't done so already, drag it into position next to the title.

4. Click on the **Swatches** tab, and change the **Fill** colour to **Scheme Colour** 1. (For details on using colour schemes, see the tutorial *Colour Schemes* on p. 125.)

5. On the **Arrange** menu, click **Anchor Object...**

6. In the **Anchored Objects Properties** dialog:

   • Select **Position inline as character**.

   • In the **Align with text** drop-down list, select **Bottom** and select the **Scale to: 100% of pointsize** option.

   • Click **OK**.

     The image is anchored to the text as an inline character.

 Anchored objects
When you anchor an object to a body of text, it remains with text at all times.

There are two ways to anchor objects in PagePlus:
• Float with text.
• Position inline as character.

For detailed information, see *Anchoring objects* in PagePlus Help.

Applying wrap settings

To finish the tutorial we'll look at wrapping text around a picture or graphic. Let's add another graphic to page 2.

To apply wrap settings:

1. On the **Pages** tab, double-click the page 2 thumbnail.

2. On the **Assets** tab, the **Graphics** category should be displayed (if not, click the header).

3. Drag the silhouette of the octopus onto the page. Notice that the frame glows to show that the graphic will be placed inside it.

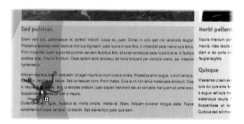

On release, the graphic is placed in the frame and the text automatically wraps around it.

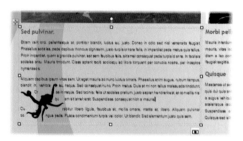

4. Click the graphic to select it and on the Arrange toolbar, click Wrap Settings.

5.   In the **Wrap Settings** dialog:

  •   In the **Wrapping** section, select **Square**.

  •   In the **Wrap To** section, select **Largest Side**.

  •   In the **Distance from text** section, enter **0.3 cm** in all four of the value boxes.

  •   Click **OK**.

6.   Drag the graphic to the right side of the frame. Notice that the text wrap updates accordingly.

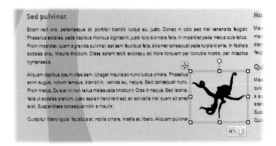

That's it! We've reached the end of this tutorial on pictures. We hope that you have enjoyed working through these simple exercises. You should be much more familiar with the techniques we've explored and able to confidently add pictures to your own publications.

Styles & Assets

The **Assets** tab in PagePlus X6 plays host to a wide variety of designs and objects to help you to easily and quickly enhance your publications. The Styles tab contains pre-defined styles so that you can also quickly add dramatic effects to text and objects. In this tutorial, we'll create a poster to see how simple it is to use the **Styles** and **Assets**.

In this tutorial, we will:

- Apply an asset background to a page.

- Place and use picture frames.

- Place graphic assets.

- Apply object styles.

Let's begin...

1. On the File menu, click New > New from Startup Wizard...

2. In the Create section, click Start New Publication.

3. In the Regular/Normal Landscape category, in the large pane, click to select the A4 or Letter thumbnail.

4. Click OK.

    A new blank document opens in the workspace.

Save now! On the File menu click Save As... In the dialog, browse to the location in which you want to save the file, type in a new name and click Save.

Using Asset Pack backgrounds

PagePlus comes with a variety of installed Asset Packs. These contain assets (objects or page elements) that can be used to quickly and efficiently build or enhance any publication.

We'll start by looking at a background asset. A background asset makes it easy to add a background design to any page. Its special properties ensure that it always fills the page area. Before you can use an asset in your publication, you need to import it into the Assets tab.

To add Background assets to the Assets tab:

1. On the Assets tab, click  Browse... to open the Asset Browser.

2. In the Categories section, click to select the Backgrounds category. The backgrounds from all installed packs are displayed in the main pane.

3. In the main pane the assets are categorized by the Pack file that they belong to. In the Grunge pack, click on the green-brown background thumbnail.

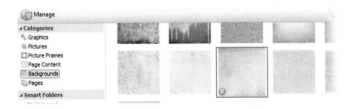

The green ⊘ shows that the asset has been added to the tab.

4. Click Close to exit.

Now that we have imported our background, we can add it to the page.

To add a background to the page:

1.   On the **Assets** tab, the **Backgrounds** category should be displayed (if not, click the header).

2.   Drag the background onto the page.

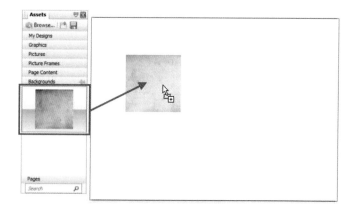

The background is added to the page as a special background layer and automatically adjusts to fit the page area.

 You can change to a different background at any time by simply dragging a different background from the **Assets** tab onto the page.

Using Picture Frame assets

Using picture frames makes it really easy to place or swap your pictures. The *Pictures* tutorial (on p. 37) discusses how to use blank frames. However, the Asset Packs contain frames with fancy borders that can really enhance your publication. We'll add one of these now.

To add Picture Frame assets to the Assets tab:

1. On the Assets tab, click ![browse icon] Browse... to open the Asset Browser.

2. In the Categories section, click to select the Picture Frames category. The picture frames from all installed packs are displayed in the main pane.

3. In the main pain the assets are categorized by the Pack file that they belong to. In the Essentials pack, click the ◎ Add All button. The assets are imported into the Assets tab.

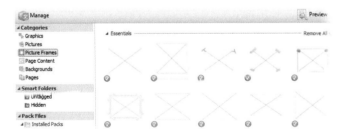

The green ◎ shows that the asset has been added to the tab.

4. Click Close to exit.

To add a picture frame to the page:

1. On the **Assets** tab, the **Picture Frames** category should be displayed (if not, click the header).

2. Scroll through the frames, select the one with push pins and then drag it onto the page.

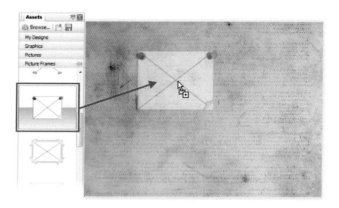

The frame is added to the page at its default size.

3. Move the frame to the right of the page and drag on the square bounding box handles to resize it so that it looks approximately like the one illustrated.

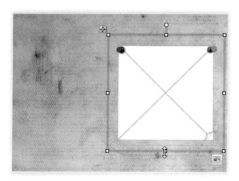

Don't forget to save your work!

We'll now add one of the installed picture assets to the frame.

To add a picture asset to the Assets tab:

1. On the **Assets** tab, click **Browse...** to open the **Asset Browser**.

2. In the **Categories** section, click to select the **Pictures** category. The images from all installed packs are displayed in the main pane.

3. In the Search box, type "tutorials".

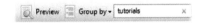

    All pictures with the "Tutorials" tag are displayed.

4. Click to select the picture of the owl and then click **Close** to exit.

To add a picture to an existing frame:

1. On the **Assets** tab, the **Pictures** category should be displayed (if not, click the header).

2. Drag the picture of the owl onto the picture frame. The picture is cropped to fit the frame boundary.

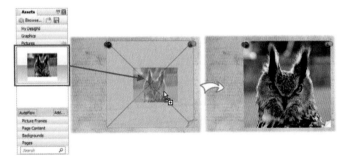

When a picture is placed inside a frame, it's easy to change the frame just by dropping a new one on top of the existing frame.

To swap a picture frame:

1. On the **Assets** tab, click the **Picture Frames** category header.

2. Drag the 'polaroid' picture thumbnail from the tab and drop it onto the owl picture. The frame is updated.

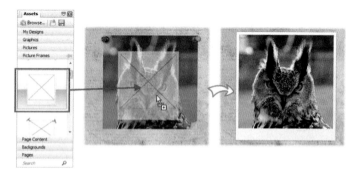

 To edit the position of the image inside the frame, use the tools on the picture frame toolbar located beneath the frame when the frame is selected. For more information, see the *Pictures* tutorial on p. 37.

 Don't forget to save your work!

Using graphic assets

Graphic assets can be used to add interest to a page. They are added to the Assets tab in exactly the same way as the other assets that we have already used.

To add graphic assets to the Assets tab:

1. On the Assets tab, click 🔍 Browse... to open the Asset Browser.

2. In the Categories section, click to select the Graphics category. The graphics from all installed packs are displayed in the main pane.

3. In the Search box, type "owl". All graphics with the "owl" tag are displayed. Click to select the first owl graphic.

The green 🟢 shows that the asset has been added to the tab.

4. In the Search box, click the cross to clear the tag. Next, type "plant" and click on one of the graphics that looks like a branch.

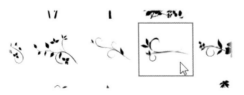

The green 🟢 shows that the asset has been added to the tab.

5. Click Close to exit.

To add a graphic to the page:

1. On the **Assets** tab, the **Graphics** category should be displayed (if not, click the header).

2. Drag the owl graphic to the page next to the picture, and then drag the branch graphic to the page. Resize and move as necessary.

Don't forget to save your work!

The page is almost finished. To complete the design we'll apply some pre-defined styles from the **Styles** tab to objects on the page.

Using the Styles tab

The **Styles** tab contains a variety of object styles (saved attributes or properties such as line colour, fill, reflections and shadows) that can be applied with a single click. You can also apply more than one type of style simultaneously. We'll look at a few of these now.

To apply a style:

1. With the ↖ **Pointer Tool**, click and drag across the page to select all of the page elements. (Alternatively, press **Ctrl** + **A** to select all.)

2. On the **Styles** tab, in the category drop-down list, select **Shadows**.

3. In the **Drop Shadow** sub-category, click on a style thumbnail to apply it.

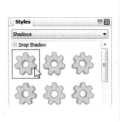 

The drop-shadow style is applied to all of the page objects.

4. Click to select only the branch, then, on the **Styles** tab, in the category drop-down list, select **Presets - Materials**.

5. Scroll down to the **Glass** sub-category and click on the first style thumbnail. The style is applied.

You can apply styles to virtually any object. To complete our design, we added some artistic text ("Bubo bubo", the scientific name for the owl) and applied the same glass-effect style. For more information about using text in PagePlus, see the tutorials *Artistic Text* on p. 25 and *Frame Text* on p. 7.

 You can also create and save your own styles for use in future publications. For more information, see PagePlus Help.

Why not apply some of these techniques to your own images? Have fun!

Logos

LogoStudio makes it easy to and edit logos in isolation from other page elements. You can create your own logos from scratch, or choose from a range of logo templates. We'll introduce you to some of the powerful LogoStudio features in this tutorial.

By the end of this tutorial you will be able to:

- Use the installed logo assets.

- Modify an existing logo.

- Create your own logo.

- Add a logo design to the Assets tab.

Let's begin...

1.   On the **File** menu, click **New > New from Startup Wizard...**

2.   In the **Create** section, click **Start New Publication**.

3.   In the dialog, select a standard page size and click **OK**.

The page opens in the workspace.

Using the Logo assets

Next, we'll have a look at adding our first logo to the page. It's time to enter LogoStudio!

 The first time you go into LogoStudio, take a moment to familiarize yourself with the layout of the tabs as they may be a little different from your normal studio layout.

To import logos to the Assets tab:

1.   On the **Assets** tab, click the **Graphics** category header and then click  Browse...

2.   In the **Asset Browser** dialog, in the search box, type "logo".

All of the pre-designed logos are displayed.

3. Click on the thumbnail of each of the logos that you want to import to the **Assets** tab.

(To import all of the logos, click 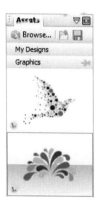Add All.)

4. When you've selected the logos you want, click **Close**.

Your selected logos will be marked and displayed in the **Graphics** category of the **Assets** tab, ready for adding to your document.

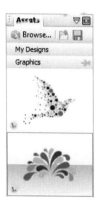

To insert a logo on the page:

1. Drag a logo from the **Graphics** category of the **Assets** tab to the page.

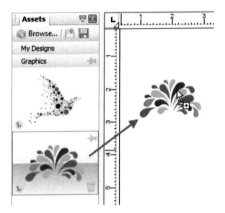

The Insert Logo dialog opens.

2. In the dialog:

    •   To apply the colour scheme of the publication, clear the **Apply colour set** check box.

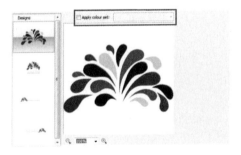

    - or -

- To apply a colour set (a specially designed logo scheme), select the **Apply colour set** check box, and then select a colour set from the drop-down list.

- In the **Designs** pane, choose your design.

- (Optional) In the **Name** text box, type your company name.

- Amend the **Motto** text.

- Click **OK**.

3. The logo is placed on the page and you can now move it into place and resize as necessary.

 Save now! On the **File** menu click **Save As...** In the dialog, browse to the location in which you want to save the file, type in a new name and click **Save**.

Editing an existing logo asset

One of the best things about the logos in PagePlus is that they're really easy to customize in order to get that tailored look for your publications. This is easily done in the LogoStudio. Let's have a look at this now.

To edit an existing logo:

1. Click the  Edit in LogoStudio button that displays on the control bar under the selected logo.

2. LogoStudio opens with your object(s) zoomed in to fit your workspace.

3. To customize your logo design, use the interactive **How To** tab elements, or the traditional PagePlus creation tools.

4. Click ⊗ **Close LogoStudio** to return to the main PagePlus workspace and view your logo on the page.

 In this logo we added a different silhouette found in the Silhouettes pack in the **Assets Browser**.

 Don't forget to save your work!

Creating your own logos

PagePlus also makes it very easy to create your own logos.

To convert an existing design to a logo:

1. Select the object(s) you want to convert to your logo.

2. On the **Tools** menu, click **Convert To > Logo...**

Your design is converted to a logo and can now be edited in LogoStudio.

 You can find the killer whale graphic in the Clipart pack in the **Assets Browser**.

To create a logo in the LogoStudio:

1. On the Insert menu, click **Logo...**

2. Click or click and drag to place the logo on the page.

The LogoStudio environment opens automatically.

3. To create your design, you can use the interactive **How To** tab elements, or the traditional PagePlus creation tools.

 To make it easier to align our objects, we clicked ▥ **Clean Design** to temporarily disable clean design mode and turn on the layout guides. This button toggles the display so if the guides are already displayed, clicking the button again will hide them.

4. To return to your original document, click  Close LogoStudio.
    Your design is displayed on page.

Don't forget to save your work!

Adding your design to the Assets tab

When you've completed you logo design, why not add it to the gallery so
that it's readily accessible for use in all of your publications?

To add a logo to the Gallery:

1. On the Gallery tab, in the category drop-down list, select My
    Designs. As you can see, we've already added a logo. If you haven't
    added anything to this category yet, it will be empty!

2. Simply drag your design into the **Assets** tab.

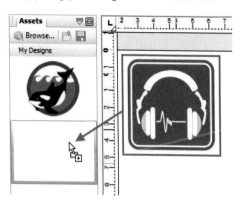

A copy of the design is displayed in the **My Designs** section of the **Assets** tab and is now ready for use in all of your future projects!

We hope that you've enjoyed this adventure into logo territory and feel confident in using them throughout your publications. Logos can be used as a great base for a nameplate design—for more information, see the online tutorial *Designing a Nameplate*. Have fun!

Master Pages

Some elements of your design will appear on every page of your publication. By using master pages, you can achieve consistency throughout your publication, and save yourself a lot of time and effort in the process!

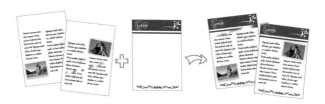

By the end of this tutorial you will be able to:

*   Create and use a master page.

*   Create a second master page.

*   Create a watermark.

*   Assign alternative master pages to a page.

To demonstrate master pages, we've created a simple tri-fold flyer, flyer.ppp, which we have provided for you. In this tutorial, we'll enhance the layout by applying a background design with a master page.

Go to **http://go.serif.com/resources/PPX6** to download the following tutorial project file(s):

flyer.ppp

Let's begin...

- On the Standard toolbar, click **Open**.

- Locate the **flyer.ppp** file and click **Open**.

  The project opens in the workspace.

Tri-fold flyer

We've already created placeholder content within this document. However, to create a tri-fold flyer from scratch:

- From the **Startup Wizard**, click **Start New Publication**.
- Click the **Folded** category and then click the **Other** sub-category.
- Click **Side Z-fold Menu**.
- Click **OK**.

Why use master pages?

Master pages are background pages, like sheets of extra paper behind your main publication pages. Every page can have a master page assigned to it and a given master page can be shared by any number of main pages.

Creating a consistent design is simple when you use a master page. When you add text frames, pictures, or other elements to the master page, they appear in the same position on all document pages that use that master page. Content placed on standard pages is displayed in front of the master page elements. This makes it easy to create a consistent design throughout your publication.

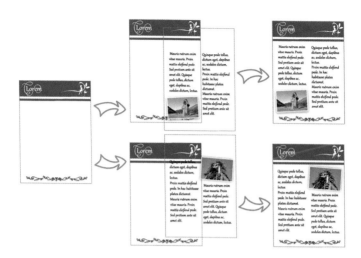

What you place on a master page is entirely up to you and often depends on the type of publication you are creating. Typical elements that you'd place on a master page include:

- background images (patterns, watermarks etc.).

- company name and/or logo.

- page number (using an automatic field—for more details, see the tutorial *Page Numbering* on p. 99).

- contact details.

Master pages simplify document maintenance as objects placed on a master page only need updating once. (If you didn't use a master page, you'd have to update the object on each individual page of the document.)

Importing the tutorial assets

For the next section of the tutorial, we'll use some of the assets found in the **Tutorials** assets pack.

To add tutorial assets to the Assets tab:

1. On the **Assets** tab, click 🔍 **Browse...** to open the **Asset Browser**.

2. In the **Pack Files** section, expand the **Tutorials** folder and click to select the **Tutorials** pack.

3. In the Search box, type "master pages". The relevant assets are displayed.

4. For each category, click the ⊘ **Add All** button. The assets are imported into the **Assets** tab.

5. Click **Close** to exit.

Creating a master page (MasterA)

Before we start, take a moment to familiarize yourself with the document layout by double-clicking the pages in the **Pages** tab.

As you can see, each page has content but it is all placed on a white background. By using a master page, we can edit all of the pages at once! Let's look at this next.

To add a background asset to a master page:

1. On the **Pages** tab, expand the **Master Pages** pane. Notice that the document currently has a single, blank master page. Let's edit this now.

2. Double-click the 'MasterA' page thumbnail to display the page in the workspace.

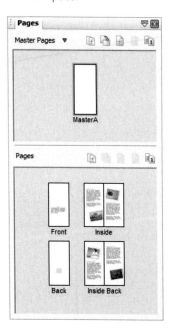

3. On the **Assets** tab, click the **Backgrounds** category.

4.   Drag the background thumbnail from the tab and onto the page.
The background is placed on a 'background' layer and automatically
resizes to match the page size.

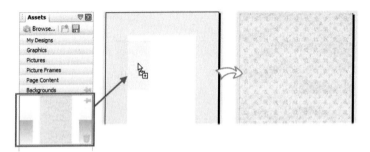

Next we'll add a couple of graphics to the page to create a more
interesting layout.

To add graphics to a master page:

1.   On the **Assets** tab, click the **Graphics** category.

2.   Drag the tall 'paper' graphic from the tab and onto the page.

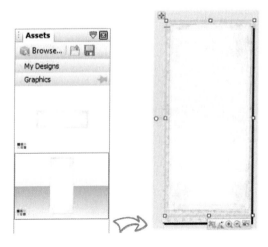

3. On the Align tab, select **Relative to: Page** and then, click  Centre Vertically and ☰ Centre Horizontally.

4. Next, drag the small 'paper' graphic from the tab and onto the page so that the top just overlaps the top edge of the tall graphic. This will hold our logo.

5. Drag the small graphic towards the horizontal centre of the page.

    A red (by default) dynamic guide will appear when the graphic is centred and a blue dynamic guide appears as you line the graphic up with the page margin.

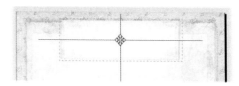

When you release the mouse button, your page should resemble ours.

Next, we'll add contact our details.

🔺 Save now! On the **File** menu click **Save As...** In the dialog, browse to the location in which you want to save the file, type in a new name and click **Save**.

To add contact details:

1. On the Tools toolbar, click the ⬛ Standard Text Frame.

2. Click and drag across the bottom of the page to place a frame approximately 8.5 cm wide and 0.5 cm high.

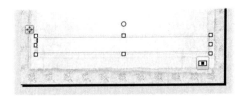

3. Go to the **Text Styles** tab and click the **Footer** paragraph style.

(If you can't see the **Footer** style, select the ⬜ Show All option.)

4.   In the text frame, type "To make an appointment call", and then on the **Insert** menu click **Information > User Details...**

5.   In the dialog, select **(Business) Phone** from the list and click **OK**. The phone number is added to the text frame.

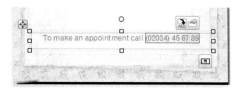

6.   Finally, drag the text frame into position at the bottom of the page.

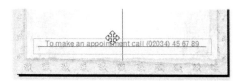

That's it, apart from our logo (which we can add at a later date) our master page is complete.

To return to normal view:

1.   Double-click a normal page thumbnail on the **Pages** tab.

2.   Click through pages on the **Pages** tab, or click the arrows on the Hintline toolbar, to view the pages.

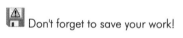 Don't forget to save your work!

Additional master pages

The design suits the inner pages well, but it looks a little boring for the cover of the folded flyer. What we need is a different design for the front and back pages. We can easily do this by creating a second master page, and we can save time and effort by reusing some of the work that we've already done!

To create a second master page:

1. On the **Pages** tab, double-click the 'MasterA' page thumbnail to display the page in the workspace.

2. Click 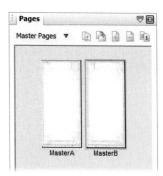 **Master Page Manager** and in the dialog:

    *   Select the **Add** tab.

    *   Select the **Copy layers from** option. The **Copy objects** option is selected by default.

    *   Click **OK**.

The duplicate master page, **MasterB**, is displayed in the workspace and as a thumbnail in the **Pages** tab.

The Add button on the Pages tab is a shortcut to adding a blank page to your document. This is ideal if you want to create an entirely different style of master page and don't need to reuse any objects.

 If you have landscape and portrait pages in your document, you can change the orientation of a master page to match.

- On the Pages tab, select the appropriate master page thumbnail.
- Click Change Page Orientation. The page updates.

Now we have our starting point, let's make some changes.

To delete multiple unwanted objects:

1. On the Tools toolbar, click the Pointer Tool.

2. Select the 'contact' text frame at the bottom of the page and press the Delete key.

To toggle Clean Design view:

- On the Arrange toolbar, click Clean Design.

When Clean Design is turned on, the button is highlighted and any guides and frame borders are hidden from view. If you have set a page bleed edge, this will be indicated by a colour fade (not visible on a white page).

To add a watermark:

1. On the Tools toolbar, in the Picture flyout, click the ⊠ Rectangular Picture Frame.

2. Click and drag on the page to place a frame within the page margin guides.

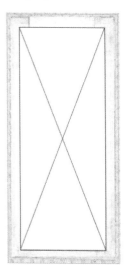

3. On the **Assets** tab, click the **Pictures** category.

4. Drag the image of the meditating woman onto the empty frame.

5. Click the Pan button and pan the image further to the right.

6. On the **Transparency** tab, click the **Solid Transparency 70%** swatch.

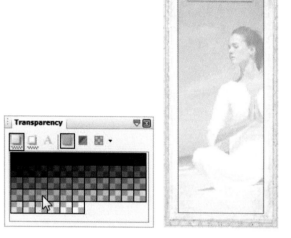

The watermark is almost complete, but for a really professional look, we'll add a tint to match the colour scheme.

7. On the **Swatches** tab, click the **Fill** button and then click **Scheme Colour 4**.

8. To darken the colour, reduce the **Tint** value to -50%.

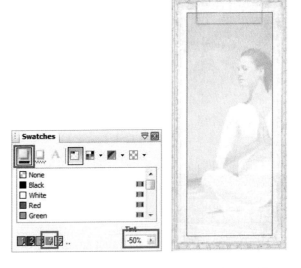

To complete the design, let's move the logo background banner to the bottom of the page.

 Don't forget to save your work!

To adjust the logo banner:

1. On the Tools toolbar, click the Pointer Tool.

2. Select the small rectangular banner and on the Arrange toolbar, click Bring to Front.

3. On the **Transform** tab, change the width to 9.5 cm. The height updates automatically as the aspect ratio is locked.

4. Finally, position the object so that the bottom edge is in line with the lower margin as illustrated.

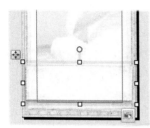

 To view the design clearly, don't forget to turn off the guides using **Clean Design** view.

To toggle Clean Design view:

- On the Arrange toolbar, click ▦ Clean Design.

Now we've completed our second master page design, we need to assign it to the front and back pages of our flyer.

To assign a master page:

1. On the **Pages** tab, double-click on the 'Front' page thumbnail to return to normal view.

2. Drag and drop the **MasterB** thumbnail onto the **Front** page thumbnail.

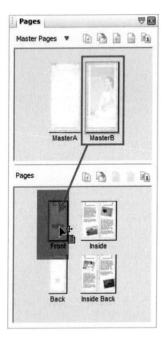

The master page is assigned.

3. Repeat step 2 and 3 to assign 'MasterB' to the 'Back' page.

To check master page assignment:

- On the **Pages** tab, click  **Show Master Page Identifiers**. The assigned master pages are displayed on each page thumbnail.

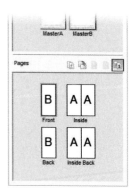

- Click the button again to return to the normal thumbnail view.

We added a modified logo to the small panel at the top of Master page A and the bottom of Master page B. For more information on how to do this, see either the How To tab, or the tutorial *Logos* on p. 65.

That's it! You have successfully created and assigned multiple master pages to a publication. Why not explore this technique in your own documents? Have fun!

 In PagePlus X6, it's also possible to assign several master pages to a single page, creating a 'layered' effect. This can be useful when you want to use some elements, e.g. a background graphic or colour, on all pages, and other elements on only certain pages of the document. Assigning multiple master pages to a page is done from the Layers tab. For a detailed look at master pages and their advanced features, see PagePlus Help.

Page Numbering

In this simple tutorial, we'll show you a useful way to combine master pages and page numbering. We'll also take a look at using mixed page number formats within a publication.

By the end of this tutorial you will be able to:

• Add page numbers to a master page.

• Promote an object from a master page.

• Create multiple sections using mixed number formats.

• Remove a page number from a specific page.

Let's begin...

1. On the **File** menu, click **New > New from Startup Wizard....**

2. In the **Create** section, click **Use Design Template**.

3. In the dialog:

    *   In the **Theme Layouts** list on the left, click the **Textured** category, then click **Vintage**.

    *   In the centre pane, select the **Brochure** template.

    *   In the **Pages** pane, select the first six pages.

    *   Click **OK**.

4. In the **User Details** dialog, make any necessary changes and click **Update**. The template opens as a new, six page document in the workspace. Each page is displayed in the **Pages** tab.

Displaying page guides and margins

To help us place the page numbers more accurately, we'll display the page guides.

To toggle Clean Design view:

* On the Arrange toolbar, click **Clean Design**.

Adding page numbers

We can easily add page numbers to every page by simply adding them to the master page(s) of our publication. PagePlus does the rest! For more information on using master pages, see the tutorial *Master Pages* on p. 77.

> You can also add a page number to a header or footer by using the Header and Footer Wizard, found in **Insert** > **Headers and Footers...** Just follow the on-screen instructions. For more information, see PagePlus Help.

To add a page number to a master page:

1. On the **Pages** tab, expand the **Master Pages** pane and double-click the 'MasterA' page thumbnail to display the page.

2. Click the **A** Artistic Text Tool, and then click once just below the bottom margin. When you release the mouse button and can see a flashing text-insertion cursor, on the **Insert** menu, click **Information** > **Page Number**.

The automatic page number is inserted.

 The actual number will correctly update when viewed on a page (and not the master page).

3. Select the page number text:

- On the Text context toolbar, format your text as desired.

- On the Text context toolbar, click the ☰ **Align Centre** button.

- On the **Align** tab, ensure **Relative to: Page** is selected and then click ⬒ **Centre Horizontally**.

 Using centred alignment on your text means that as your page number extends from 1 to 2 to 3 characters, the entire number will remain centred.

4. On the **Pages** tab, click each of the page thumbnails to display them in the workspace.

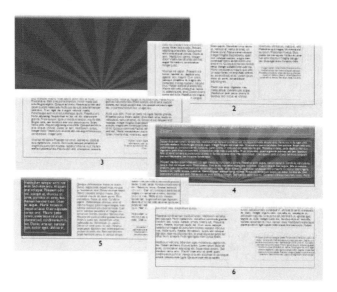

As you can see, the page number is displayed in the same place at the bottom of each page, with one exception, page 1. This is because there is a blue object that has been placed on that page. However, in this instance, we can easily fix this by "promoting" the page number from the master page.

Save now! On the **File** menu click **Save As...** In the dialog, browse to the location in which you want to save the file, type in a new name and click **Save**.

Promoting objects from a master page

If you want to apply different formatting to a master page object without affecting the other pages that use the master page, you can do this by "promoting" the object. This essentially places a copy the object onto the current page, and hides the original master page object from view. You can then change the copy in any way without affecting the overall document.

Let's have a go at this now.

 The next steps can be completed using any object placed on a master page.

To promote an object from a master page:

1. In the **Pages** tab, double-click the Page 1 thumbnail. The page is displayed in the workspace.

2. Starting with the Pointer on the workspace just off the page, click and drag to create a selection around the approximate position of the page number. If you don't succeed the first time, try a larger selection area.

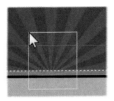

The page number object is selected.

3.   Click Promote from Master Page.

4.   With the object still selected, on the Arrange toolbar, click **Bring to Front**.

5.   On the **Swatches** tab, ensure the **Text** button is selected and click a light coloured swatch. The text is updated and can be easily seen on the front page.

 Don't forget to save your work!

Special and mixed page number formats

In larger publications, it's common to see different styles of page numbers for different sections. For example, the contents pages may have roman numerals while the main body of the publication will have an arabic (standard) format. We'll briefly show you how to do this with the **Page Number Format** dialog.

To create publication page number sections:

1. On the **Format** menu, click **Page Number Format...**

2. On the lower left side of the dialog, beneath the **Section** pane, click **Add...**

3. In the **Add New Section** dialog, type the number "2" to start the new section at page 2 and click **OK**.

4. Repeat the step, this time starting the new section at page 4. Your dialog should resemble ours.

Section	
Pages	Format
1	1
2 - 3	2 - 3
4 - 6	4 - 6

Before we exit the dialog, we'll reformat our second section.

To format page numbers:

1. In the **Section** pane, in the **Pages** column, click page 2-3.

2. In the **Style** pane, select **Lower Roman i, ii, iii, ...**

   The format updates.

Pages	Format
1	1
2 - 3	ii - iii
4 - 6	4 - 6

3.   In the Numbering section, clear the **Continue from previous section** option and type the number "1" (one) as your **First page number** (the format will update automatically when you click away from the input box).

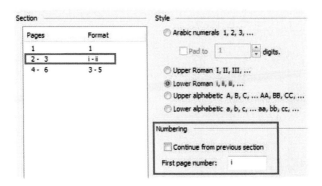

4.   In the **Section** pane, in the **Pages** column, click page 4-6, and in the Numbering section, clear the **Continue from previous section** option and type "1" (one) as your **First page number**. Leave the formatting set to **Arabic numerals** 1, 2, 3, ...

Once again, the section numbers are updated.

Pages	Format
1	1
2 - 3	i - ii
4 - 6	1 - 3

5.   Click OK to exit the dialog.

On the **Pages** tab, you'll see that the numbering beneath the thumbnails has updated to show the new sections.

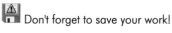 Don't forget to save your work!

Removing page numbers from a single page

In a publication using the number styling we've created, it would be common practice not to see a number on the first page. In an earlier step, we promoted the number from the master page so that we could see it. In the same way, once an object has been promoted from a master page, we can also delete it without affecting the other pages.

To "delete" a promoted master page object:

1. Select the object to delete, in our case the page number. The **Revert to Master Page** button beneath the object shows that it is no longer associated to the master page.

2. Press the **Delete** key. The object is removed from the first page.

If you now view each page, you'll see how the numbers change in each section.

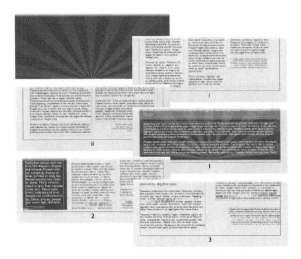

When subsequent pages are added to your publication, they will use the number formatting assigned to the previous page.

 The recommended way to add new pages to a section is to display the last page of the section in the workspace, and then use the **Page Manager** to add additional pages after your selected page. For more information, see PagePlus Help.

 Don't forget to save your work!

(Optional) Creating event tickets

Now that you know how to format page numbers, why not combine this with a 'small publication' document and automatically create sequentially numbered tickets? You could easily create individually numbered tickets for fund raisers, music gigs, club and sports events, and more.

The possibilities are endless! Here is an example that is designed to be printed on standard business card paper to get you started.

 The entire ticket design is done on the master page of the **Wide Business Card** new publication type. When your design is complete, simply insert the number of pages that you wish to print so that the 'ticket' numbers increase automatically.

The ticket body:

* We used **Artistic text** for the main text (A) and formatted it appropriately with the **Swatches** tab and the Text context toolbar.

* To create visual interest, we used a silhouette graphic **asset** and applied a red fill (B).

* A text frame was used for the general ticket information (E) and formatted with the **Swatches** tab and the Text context toolbar.

* We placed a text frame object and inserted a page number (**Insert > Information > Page Number**) to create the ticket number (F). In the **Page Number Format** dialog, we set **Pad to 4 digits** (see note).

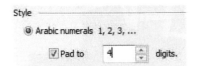

You can prefix your automatic numbering with leading zeros using the **Page Number Format** option.

• In the **Page Number Format** dialog, select the **Pad to** option and enter the number of digits you want the number to be. (For example, for numbers between 1 and 9999, pad to 4 digits.)

• Click OK. All page numbers below the set number of digits will be displayed with the correct number of leading zeros.

The ticket stub:

• We added a line and formatted it on the **Line** tab to create the stub separator.

• To create visual interest, we used a silhouette graphic **asset** and applied a red fill (D).

• To create the ticket stub number (C), we replicated the previous ticket number (F), and then rotated the frame by 90° and increased the size of the text.

• We replicated the main text objects (A) and rotated and reduced them to fit our stub (G).

Tables

Tables are a great way of displaying all forms of data quickly and easily. They can also be used as layout tools. Price lists, menus, general lists, school timetables, research data, opening times—all look best when inserted into a table on your publication. The best part is that PagePlus makes this easy to do.

In this tutorial, we'll show you how to:

*   Create a table.

*   Populate a table with data.

*   Add and delete rows and columns.

*   Format the appearance of your table.

In this tutorial, we are going to add a price list to the back of a health spa flyer. To help you follow the tutorial, we've provided our file for you.

Go to **http://go.serif.com/resources/PPX6** to download the following tutorial project file(s):

🟠 flyer2.ppp

Let's begin...

- On the Standard toolbar, click 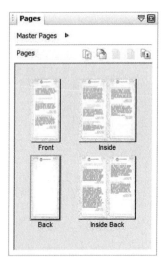 **Open**.

- Browse to the **flyer2.ppp** file, click to select it and then click **Open**.

  The publication opens in the PagePlus workspace.

- On the **Pages** tab, double-click on the 'Back' page to display it.

Displaying page guides and margins

To help us to place the table more accurately, we'll temporarily display the page guides.

To toggle Clean Design view:

- On the Arrange toolbar, click 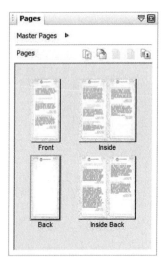 Clean Design.

Creating a table

We're ready to add our table.

To create a table:

1. On the Tools toolbar, click the 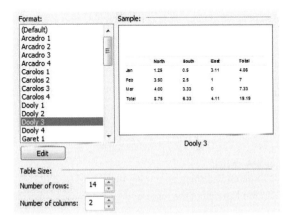 Table Tool.

2. Position your mouse pointer over the left margin guide, just below the logo banner. Click and drag to create a table the length of the page, between the margin guides.

3. In the Create Table dialog:

    *   In the Format list, click Dooly 3.

    *   Set the Number of rows to 14.

    *   Set the Number of columns to 2.

    *   Click OK.

The two column table is added to our page.

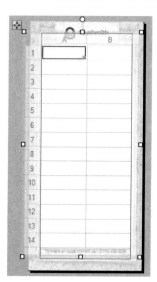

Save now! On the **File** menu click **Save As...** In the dialog, browse to the location in which you want to save the file, type in a new name and click **Save**.

Populating the table

Let's now add our information to the table.

To add table data:

1. Click in the first cell of the table and type the word 'Treatment'.

2. Click in the next header cell and type 'Price'.

3. Press the right arrow. Notice that the cursor goes to the next available cell. Type 'Aromatherapy', and press the right arrow to move to the next cell.

4. Type '£65'.

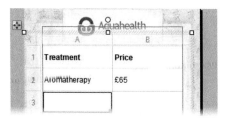

5. Complete the table using the treatments found in the flyer. (If you don't want to do this, simply add some text to the next 10 frames!)

Don't forget to save your work!

Modifying the table

Now that we've added all of the treatments, you'll notice that we have
two rows left over. As they're not needed, we can delete them.

To delete table row(s) :

1. Click inside the first cell that you want to delete and then drag over
    the other three empty cells.

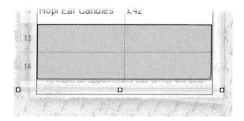

2. On the **Table** menu, click **Delete** > **Row(s)**.

3. The rows are deleted from the table.

We'll now show you how to add a column to your table.

To add a column:

1. With your table selected, click on the column header **B**. The whole
    column is highlighted.

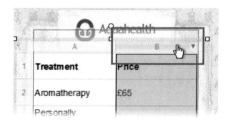

2. On the **Table** menu, click **Insert** > **Columns....**

3. In the dialog, select the **After selected cells** option and click **OK.**

A new column is added to the right of the table.

To resize a column:

1. With your table selected, click on the column header **B.**

2. Position the pointer on the divide between column headers **B** and **C.**

3. Drag to the left to reduce the width of column B so that the word 'Price' just fits.

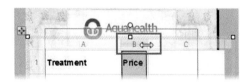

4. In the heading row of column C, type 'Duration'. Don't worry if the formatting is different, we'll fix this in a minute.

5.   Click on column header C to select the column.

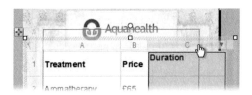

6.   On the **Table** menu, click **Autofit to Contents > Column(s)**.

7.   Finally, drag the right-centre handle of the table to the right so that it fits to the page margin again.

Now that the table fits nicely on the page, type the treatment duration information into the new column that you created.

Treatment	Price	Duration
Aromatherapy	£65	55 mins
Personally Prescribed Aromatherapy	£80	85 mins
Detoxifying Seaweed Wrap	£52	55 mins

 Don't forget to save your work!

Formatting the table

You'll notice that the formatting is slightly different to that in the first two columns. We can fix this by re-applying the table **Auto Format**.

To apply table Auto Format:

1. Click on the table to select it.

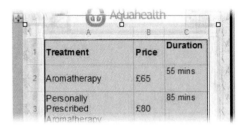

2. On the Table context toolbar, click 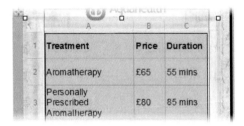 **Auto Format**.

3. In the **AutoFormat** dialog, in the **Format** pane, click **Dooly 3** and then click **OK**.

The table format is reapplied.

To create a custom table format:

1. On the **Table** menu, click **Edit AutoFormat...**

    The **Table Formats** dialog opens, ready to edit the currently applied table format.

2. In the **Cell Style** pane, click **Odd Row** and then click **Edit...**

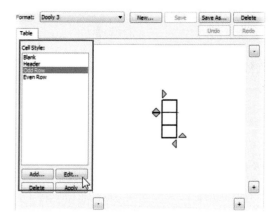

3. In the **Cell Properties** dialog:

    *   Click the **Font** tab.

    *   In the **Font** drop-down list, select **Life BT**.

    *   In the **Size** drop-down list, select **9 pt**.

    *   Click **OK**.

        The changes are displayed in the Preview pane.

4. In the **Cell Style** pane, click **Even Row** and then click **Edit...** and repeat step 3.

5. In the **Cell Style** pane, click **Header** and then click **Edit...**

6. In the **Cell Properties** dialog:

- Click the **Font** tab.

- In the **Font** drop-down list, select **Life BT**.

- Click **OK**.

7. Click **Save As...**

8. Type a name for your new format, for example 'Flyer', and click **OK**.

9. Finally, click **OK** to close the **Table Formats** dialog.

Your table is updated with the new format.

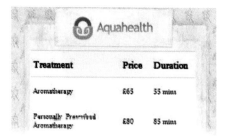

 For this screenshot, we re-enabled Clean Design by clicking the button on the Arrange toolbar.

By formatting the table in this way, you will be able to quickly apply this style to any table in future publications with the **Auto Format** button on the Table context toolbar.

Don't forget to save your work!

Tables, tables everywhere!

There are many more things that you can do with table formatting, for example, you can change cell colour to match your publication and create your own from scratch. You can also add inline images as in the product list example.

Why not create your own calendar with the **Calendar Tool**? The formatting techniques are very similar and a Wizard will guide you through the initial setup.

Although beyond the scope of this tutorial, you'll find more information in the PagePlus Help and on the **How To** tab. Have fun!

Colour Schemes

When designing your publications, one of the most important factors to consider is colour. It sets the mood, sends a message and gets attention. But how do you select a colour palette that's right for your publication? In the first of the colour schemes tutorials, we'll introduce you to PagePlus colour schemes.

In the first section of this tutorial, we'll apply scheme colours to individual elements on a page. We'll then show you how you can edit and modify scheme colours.

By the end of this tutorial you will be able to:

- Apply a preset colour scheme.

- Apply schemed colours to objects.

- Modify an existing colour scheme.

- Save a modified scheme.

Let's begin...

1.   On the File menu, click New > New from Startup Wizard....

2.   In the Create section, click Use Design Template.

3.   In the dialog:

  •   In the Address labels list on the left, click the Small Address
      Label category.

  •   In the centre pane, select the Doodle template.

  •   Click OK.

      The page opens in the workspace.

Applying alternative colour schemes

Many of the elements on this page have been designed to use colour schemes. Let's look at this now by choosing a different scheme.

To apply a colour scheme:

1. At the bottom-right of the studio, click **Schemes** to expand the **Schemes** tab.

    You'll see an assortment of named schemes, each consisting of five basic colours. The colour scheme that is currently applied is highlighted.

2. On the **Schemes** tab, click to select **Scheme 3**.

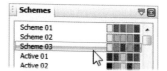

All schemed objects within the publication update with the new colours.

 If you take a look at our design templates, you'll notice that these are also designed to use colour schemes so that you can change the look and feel quickly and easily.

Applying scheme colours to objects

The scheme colours work much like a paint-by-numbers system, where various regions and elements of a page layout are coded with numbers. In each scheme, a specific colour is assigned to each number. You can change or even apply a colour scheme at any point during the design process, but it's best practice to scheme your objects from the start. This gives you the most flexibility if you decide to change the look and feel of a publication.

 A publication can only have one colour scheme in use at any given time.

To apply a scheme colour to an object:

1. On the Tools toolbar, on the ▢⁻ QuickShape flyout, click the
    ❀ Quick Petal and draw a large shape on the page.

2. Click to display the Swatches tab.

At the bottom of the tab, below the colour swatches, you'll see that the five main colours of the current colour scheme appear as numbered swatches.

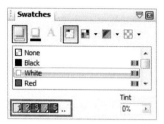

3. Ensure that the shape is selected and on the **Swatches** tab:

   - Click the ⬜ Fill button and then click the scheme colour you want to apply to the shape's fill.

   - Click the ⬜ Line button and apply a different scheme colour to the shape's outline.

4. On the **Schemes** tab, click to apply a different colour scheme to the publication. PagePlus applies the new scheme colours to the shape.

On the **Swatches** tab, notice that the colour scheme swatches have been replaced with the new scheme colours.

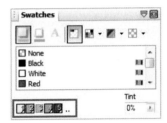

You can also apply scheme colours to text in the same way.

As you can see, when you create new elements in any publication, you can extend a colour scheme to your layout elements using the process just described.

 If you copy an object that uses scheme colours to another PagePlus publication, the object will take on the colour scheme used in the new document.

You'll need to spend some time working out which colour combinations look best, but the mechanics of the process are simple.

Save now! On the **File** menu click **Save As...** In the dialog, browse to the location in which you want to save the file, type in a new name and click **Save**.

Modifying colour schemes

If you've tried various colour schemes but haven't found one that's quite right for your document, you can modify any of the colours in an existing scheme to create a new one.

To modify a colour scheme:

1. On the **Swatches** tab click the ·· button (next to the colour swatches).

2. In the **Colour Scheme Designer** dialog, the current scheme colours are displayed.

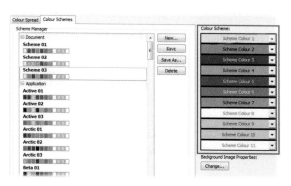

Each of the five main scheme colours (plus 6 additional colours) has its own drop-down list, showing available colours.

3.   To set or change a scheme colour, simply click the button to expand the drop-down list, and then select a new colour.

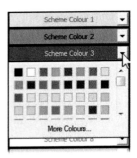

4.   (Optional) If the drop-down palette doesn't contain the colour you want to use, click **More Colours** to display the **Colour Selector**.

In the **Colour Selector** dialog, various controls allow you to choose a colour to apply or mix your own custom colours.

•   The **Models** tab displays the colour space of the currently selected colour model.

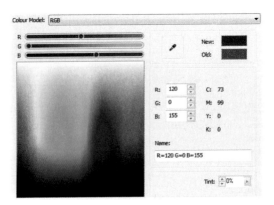

- The **Publication Palette** colour mode lets you modify the set of colours associated with the current publication.

- Click **OK** to save changes and exit the dialog.

5. When you have modified your scheme, click **OK** to apply it to your publication.

Don't forget to save your work!

Saving a modified scheme

When you save your document, its current colour scheme is saved with the publication. However, if you want to use the scheme in other publications, you need to save it to the application. (To learn how to create and modify your colour schemes, see the tutorial *Colour Schemes II: Custom Schemes* on p. 137.)

To save a scheme (application):

1. On the **Swatches** tab click the ·· button and ensure that the **Colour Schemes** tab is displayed.

2. In the **Colour Scheme** pane, the current document scheme colours are displayed.

3. To create a new scheme, click **Save As...** and type in a new name and click OK.

- or -

To overwrite an existing scheme, click to select it and then, click Save.

4. The scheme library is updated to reflect the changes. If you have created a new scheme, it will appear at the bottom of the Application list.

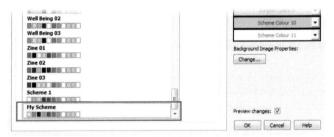

In future, you will be able to load your saved scheme from within any project.

There are two types of colour scheme—**Document** and **Application**—that are saved in the library. An Application colour scheme is saved globally and can be loaded (applied) to any publication. A Document colour scheme is template specific and is only available within a publication created from that template. However, you can save a copy of a Document (template) scheme as an application scheme if you want to use it in any other publication.

When a scheme is loaded, a copy of it is created as your publication scheme. You can modify this as much as you want and the changes will be saved with you publication. However, any changes you make will not update the Application scheme unless you explicitly choose to overwrite it.

For more information, see PagePlus Help.

Colour Schemes II: Custom Schemes

There may be times when you want to create a new colour scheme from scratch, perhaps using colours from your company logo or an image that features in your PagePlus document or on your website. Creating a colour scheme that complements your images is also a good design technique.

By the end of this tutorial you will be able to:

- Select suitable scheme colours from an image.

- Create and save a new colour scheme.

- Create a colour scheme from a base colour.

Let's begin...

1. On the **File** menu, click **New** > **New from Startup Wizard...**

2. In the **Create** section, click **Start New Publication**.

3. In the dialog, select a standard landscape page size and click **OK**.

    The page opens in the workspace.

Creating custom colour schemes from scratch

In PagePlus, there are two ways of creating a colour scheme, automatically starting with a base colour, or by choosing your colours from an image.

 You can use our sample photograph or any image of your choice. You'll find the sample picture if you browse the **Images** pack in the **Assets** tab Asset Browser. (For more about using the **Assets** tab, see PagePlus Help.)

Choosing your scheme colours from an image

One of the best ways of designing a colour scheme for your publication is to base it around the images that you've used. This way, it will tie all of the design elements together. We'll show you how to do this now.

To create colour scheme placeholders:

1. Add your image to the page and resize it so that there is some white space around it.

2. On the Tools toolbar, on the QuickShapes flyout, click the **Quick Rectangle**.

3. Draw a small square on the page next to the image.

4. With the shape still selected, on the **Edit** menu, click **Replicate...**

5. In the **Replicate** dialog:

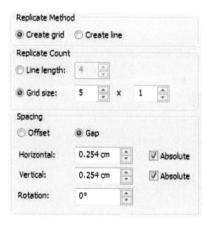

- In the **Replicate Method** section, click **Create grid**.

- In the **Replicate Count** section, set the **Grid size** to 5 wide by 1 high.

- Set the **Spacing** to **Gap** (we used the default setting of 0.254cm) and ensure that the **Absolute** checkbox is selected.

  The preview updates.

- Click **OK**.

  The squares have been replicated and aligned next to the image.

Next, we need to prepare our image and start choosing the colours for our scheme. First, we'll apply a filter to reduce the available colours, and then we'll use the colour picker to select individual colours.

To select colours from an image:

1. Select the image and then on the Picture context toolbar, click ⓢ PhotoLab.

2. In **PhotoLab**, click the **Effects** tab and then expand the **Style** category. Click the **Pixelate** thumbnail.

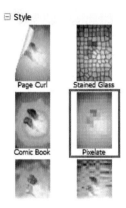

⊟ Style

Page Curl   Stained Glass

Comic Book   Pixelate

In the lower right **Trial Zone**, the **Pixelate** control displays.

Trial Zone   ⓢ Commit

▽ ▣ Pixelate   ⬚ ▾ ↰ ☒

Cell Size: 50 pix

3. Drag the **Cell Size** slider, so that colours making up the image blend into colour 'blocks,' as illustrated. You don't want the blocks either too large or too small. We found **80 pix** worked well.

Click **Commit** when you are happy with the result.

4. To close **PhotoLab** and return to the PagePlus workspace, click OK.

5. Back on the page, select the first square you created, click the Colour tab, and then click the ✦ **Colour Picker**.

6. On the image, click and drag to select the first colour you want to add to your new colour scheme. Ideally, start with the darkest colour.

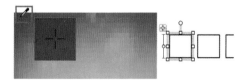

The popup colour sample updates as you drag to different areas of the image. When you are happy with the colour displayed in the sample, release the mouse button.

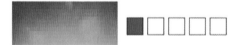

The selected colour is applied to the square, and added to the
Publication Palette on the Swatches tab.

7.   Selecting each of the remaining squares in turn, repeat the previous
step to fill the shapes with four additional colours from your image.

8.   On the Swatches tab, scroll to the end of the palette swatches to find
your new custom colours displayed.

Save now! On the File menu click Save As... In the dialog, browse
to the location in which you want to save the file, type in a new name
and click Save.

Creating and saving the scheme

We're now ready to create our new colour scheme.

To create a scheme from selected colours:

1. On the **Swatches** tab, click ·· to open the **Colour Scheme Designer**.

2. In the Colour Scheme pane:

   - Click the arrow next to **Scheme Colour 1** to expand the drop-down palette.

   - Locate the colours you added in the previous steps.

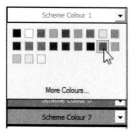

   - Click the colour you want to assign to **Scheme Colour 1**.

   The colour is applied.

3. Repeat step 2 to assign the remaining scheme colours.

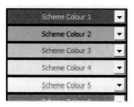

4. Ensure you have the **Colour Schemes** tab selected and then:

- Click **Save**, to update the globally available named scheme with the newly defined scheme, and apply the scheme to the publication.

- Click **Save As...** then name your scheme in the dialog and click OK. This creates a new globally available named scheme from the newly defined scheme, and applies the scheme to the publication.

5. Click OK to exit the **Colour Scheme Designer**, apply the defined scheme to the publication and store it locally.

6. Click the **Swatches** tab. Note that the swatches at the bottom of the tab now display your custom scheme colours.

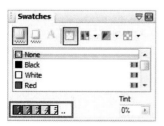

You can use these swatches to apply scheme colours to objects on your page.

Creating a scheme from a base colour

If you have a basic colour in mind for your publication, but you're not sure which colours to use with it, let the **Colour Scheme Designer** do all the hard work! We're still going to start with a colour picked from the same image, but you can pick up your colour from anywhere!

Creating a scheme using the Colour Scheme Designer:

1. Add your image to the page and on the **Swatches** tab, click ·· to open the **Colour Scheme Designer**.

2. Click the **Colour Spread** tab.

3. Click and drag the ✐ **Colour Picker**, choose your base colour from the image. This should be suitable for the 'middle' colour of the new scheme, not too light or too dark.

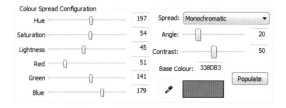

4. Select a spread type from the **Spread** drop-down list. These are based on standard Colour Theory principles. We selected **Monochromatic**.

5. (Optional) Increase the **Contrast** to increase the range in the colours. Change the **Angle** to alter where the colours are picked up from the colour wheel.

6. Click **Populate**.

- or -

For more control, click and drag the individual colour swatches onto a specific Scheme colour.

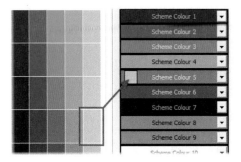

7. Click the **Colour Schemes** tab and then click **Save As...** Name your scheme in the dialog and click **OK**.

8. If you are happy with your colour scheme, click **OK** to exit the **Colour Scheme Designer**.

9. Click the **Swatches** tab. Note that the swatches at the bottom of the tab now display your custom scheme colours.

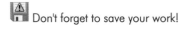 Don't forget to save your work!

Congratulations, you've created a custom colour scheme from scratch! It's a relatively simple process, but one which we hope you'll find useful in your future PagePlus publications. For more information on the Colour Scheme Designer, see PagePlus Help.

For more information on using colour schemes in your publication, see the tutorial *Colour Schemes* on p. 125.

Have fun experimenting!

Theme Layouts

PagePlus provides a selection of **Theme Layout** templates that you can use as starting points for your own publications. We've even provided placeholders for your own images!

Theme Layouts templates are split into the following style categories- **Editorial**, **Graphical**, **Illustrative** and **Textured**. There are 40 different themes, each containing over 20 different document types which cover a wide range of layout styles. With this amount of choice, you're bound to find the right layout for your needs!

- Address Labels
- Brochures
- Business Cards
- Business Forms
- Compliment Slips
- Emails

- Envelopes
- Letterheads
- Newsletters
- Flyers
- Logos
- Posters

To open a Theme Layout template:

1 In the Startup Wizard, in the **Create** section click **Use Design Template**.

2 In the **Choose a Design Template** dialog:

   • Select **Theme Layouts**.

   • Choose a theme layout category and then select a theme from the list.

   • In the adjacent pane, click a thumbnail to select a document type.

   • In the upper-right drop-down list, choose a document colour

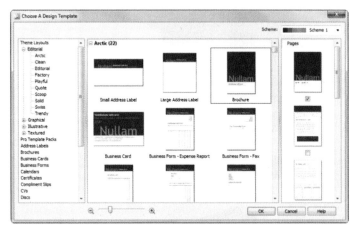

   scheme (you can always change your mind later).

   • In the rightmost pane, select the pages to include in the layout.

   • Click **OK**.

   The layouts are added as pages to your new publication.

The following pages provide previews of the **Theme Layout** templates provided with **PagePlus X6**.

Arctic

- Brochure
- Letterhead
- Compliment Slip
- Business Cards
- Address Labels

- Expense Report
- Memorandum
- Fax Transmittal
- Inventory List
- Invoice
- Time Billing
- Quotation
- Purchase Order

- Newsletter
- Envelopes
- Flyers
- Posters

Asset Pack includes:

- 6 Graphics
- 13 Photo Frames
- 19 Page Content items

- 2 Backgrounds
- 3 Pages

Clean

- Brochure
- Letterhead
- Compliment Slip
- Business Cards
- Address Labels

- Expense Report
- Memorandum
- Fax Transmittal
- Inventory List
- Invoice
- Time Billing
- Quotation
- Purchase Order

- Newsletter
- Envelopes
- Flyers
- Posters

Asset Pack includes:

- 5 Graphics
- 3 Photo Frames
- 20 Page Content items

- 2 Backgrounds
- 3 Pages

Editorial

- Brochure
- Letterhead
- Compliment Slip
- Business Cards
- Address Labels

- Expense Report
- Memorandum
- Fax Transmittal
- Inventory List
- Invoice
- Time Billing
- Quotation
- Purchase Order

- Newsletter
- Envelopes
- Flyers
- Posters

Asset Pack includes:

- 3 Graphics
- 8 Photo Frames
- 7 Page Content items
- 2 Backgrounds
- 3 Pages

Factory

- Brochure
- Letterhead
- Compliment Slip
- Business Cards
- Address Labels

- Expense Report
- Memorandum
- Fax Transmittal
- Inventory List
- Invoice
- Time Billing
- Quotation
- Purchase Order

- Newsletter
- Envelopes
- Flyers
- Posters

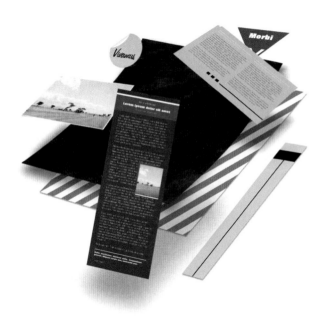

Asset Pack includes:

- 30 Graphics
- 10 Photo Frames
- 10 Page Content items
- 2 Backgrounds
- 2 Pages

Playful

- Brochure
- Letterhead
- Compliment Slip
- Business Cards
- Address Labels

- Expense Report
- Memorandum
- Fax Transmittal
- Inventory List
- Invoice
- Time Billing
- Quotation
- Purchase Order

- Newsletter
- Envelopes
- Flyers
- Posters

Asset Pack includes:

- 12 Graphics
- 4 Photo Frames
- 11 Page Content items

- 2 Backgrounds
- 2 Pages

Quote

- Brochure
- Letterhead
- Compliment Slip
- Business Cards
- Address Labels

- Expense Report
- Memorandum
- Fax Transmittal
- Inventory List
- Invoice
- Time Billing
- Quotation
- Purchase Order

- Newsletter
- Envelopes
- Flyers
- Posters

Asset Pack includes:

- 18 Graphics
- 7 Photo Frames
- 23 Page Content items
- 2 Backgrounds
- 3 Pages

Scoop

- Brochure
- Letterhead
- Compliment Slip
- Business Cards
- Address Labels

- Expense Report
- Memorandum
- Fax Transmittal
- Inventory List
- Invoice
- Time Billing
- Quotation
- Purchase Order

- Newsletter
- Envelopes
- Flyers
- Posters

Asset Pack includes:

- 18 Graphics
- 8 Photo Frames
- 7 Page Content items
- 2 Backgrounds
- 2 Pages

Solid

- Brochure
- Letterhead
- Compliment Slip
- Business Cards
- Address Labels

- Expense Report
- Memorandum
- Fax Transmittal
- Inventory List
- Invoice
- Time Billing
- Quotation
- Purchase Order

- Newsletter
- Envelopes
- Flyers
- Posters

Asset Pack includes:

- 9 Graphics
- 9 Photo Frames
- 13 Page Content items
- 2 Backgrounds
- 2 Pages

Swiss

- Brochure
- Letterhead
- Compliment Slip
- Business Cards
- Address Labels

- Expense Report
- Memorandum
- Fax Transmittal
- Inventory List
- Invoice
- Time Billing
- Quotation
- Purchase Order

- Newsletter
- Envelopes
- Flyers
- Posters

Asset Pack includes:

- 12 Graphics
- 9 Photo Frames
- 15 Page Content items

- 2 Backgrounds
- 3 Pages

Trendy

- Brochure
- Letterhead
- Compliment Slip
- Business Cards
- Address Labels

- Expense Report
- Memorandum
- Fax Transmittal
- Inventory List
- Invoice
- Time Billing
- Quotation
- Purchase Order

- Newsletter
- Envelopes
- Flyers
- Posters

Asset Pack includes:

- 5 Graphics
- 9 Photo Frames
- 12 Page Content items
- 2 Backgrounds
- 3 Pages

Active

- Brochure
- Letterhead
- Compliment Slip
- Business Cards
- Address Labels

- Expense Report
- Memorandum
- Fax Transmittal
- Inventory List
- Invoice
- Time Billing
- Quotation
- Purchase Order

- Newsletter
- Envelopes
- Flyers
- Posters

Asset Pack includes:

- 14 Graphics
- 7 Photo Frames
- 18 Page Content items
- 2 Backgrounds
- 3 Pages

Beta

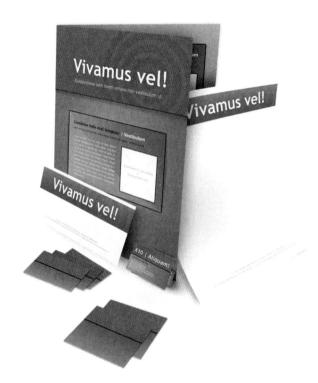

- Brochure
- Letterhead
- Compliment Slip
- Business Cards
- Address Labels

- Expense Report
- Memorandum
- Fax Transmittal
- Inventory List
- Invoice
- Time Billing
- Quotation
- Purchase Order

- Newsletter
- Envelopes
- Flyers
- Posters

Asset Pack includes:

- 7 Graphics
- 7 Photo Frames
- 22 Page Content items
- 2 Backgrounds
- 3 Pages

Dribble

- Brochure
- Letterhead
- Compliment Slip
- Business Cards
- Address Labels

- Expense Report
- Memorandum
- Fax Transmittal
- Inventory List
- Invoice
- Time Billing
- Quotation
- Purchase Order

- Newsletter
- Envelopes
- Flyers
- Posters

Asset Pack includes:

- 25 Graphics
- 8 Photo Frames
- 14 Page Content items
- 2 Backgrounds
- 2 Pages

Healthy

- Brochure
- Letterhead
- Compliment Slip
- Business Cards
- Address Labels

- Expense Report
- Memorandum
- Fax Transmittal
- Inventory List
- Invoice
- Time Billing
- Quotation
- Purchase Order

- Newsletter
- Envelopes
- Flyers
- Posters

Asset Pack includes:

- 16 Graphics
- 6 Photo Frames
- 21 Page Content items

- 2 Backgrounds
- 3 Pages

Stitch

- Brochure
- Letterhead
- Compliment Slip
- Business Cards
- Address Labels

- Expense Report
- Memorandum
- Fax Transmittal
- Inventory List
- Invoice
- Time Billing
- Quotation
- Purchase Order

- Newsletter
- Envelopes
- Flyers
- Posters

Asset Pack includes:

- 20 Graphics
- 10 Photo Frames
- 29 Page Content items

- 2 Backgrounds
- 3 Pages

Supple

- Brochure
- Letterhead
- Compliment Slip
- Business Cards
- Address Labels

- Expense Report
- Memorandum
- Fax Transmittal
- Inventory List
- Invoice
- Time Billing
- Quotation
- Purchase Order

- Newsletter
- Envelopes
- Flyers
- Posters

Asset Pack includes:

- 28 Graphics
- 10 Photo Frames
- 21 Page Content items

- 2 Backgrounds
- 4 Pages

Sylvan

- Brochure
- Letterhead
- Compliment Slip
- Business Cards
- Address Labels

- Expense Report
- Memorandum
- Fax Transmittal
- Inventory List
- Invoice
- Time Billing
- Quotation
- Purchase Order

- Newsletter
- Envelopes
- Flyers
- Posters

Asset Pack includes:

- 15 Graphics
- 9 Photo Frames
- 17 Page Content items
- 2 Backgrounds
- 4 Pages

Tabs

- Brochure
- Letterhead
- Compliment Slip
- Business Cards
- Address Labels

- Expense Report
- Memorandum
- Fax Transmittal
- Inventory List
- Invoice
- Time Billing
- Quotation
- Purchase Order

- Newsletter
- Envelopes
- Flyers
- Posters

Asset Pack includes:

- 15 Graphics
- 6 Photo Frames
- 14 Page Content items

- 2 Backgrounds
- 3 Pages

Well Being

- Brochure
- Letterhead
- Compliment Slip
- Business Cards
- Address Labels

- Expense Report
- Memorandum
- Fax Transmittal
- Inventory List
- Invoice
- Time Billing
- Quotation
- Purchase Order

- Newsletter
- Envelopes
- Flyers
- Posters

Asset Pack includes:

- 12 Graphics
- 11 Photo Frames
- 13 Page Content items

- 2 Backgrounds
- 2 Pages

Boxes

- Brochure
- Letterhead
- Compliment Slip
- Business Cards
- Address Labels

- Expense Report
- Memorandum
- Fax Transmittal
- Inventory List
- Invoice
- Time Billing
- Quotation
- Purchase Order

- Newsletter
- Envelopes
- Flyers
- Posters

Asset Pack includes:

- 10 Graphics
- 9 Photo Frames
- 12 Page Content items

- 2 Backgrounds
- 4 Pages

Globes

- Brochure
- Letterhead
- Compliment Slip
- Business Cards
- Address Labels

- Expense Report
- Memorandum
- Fax Transmittal
- Inventory List
- Invoice
- Time Billing
- Quotation
- Purchase Order

- Newsletter
- Envelopes
- Flyers
- Posters

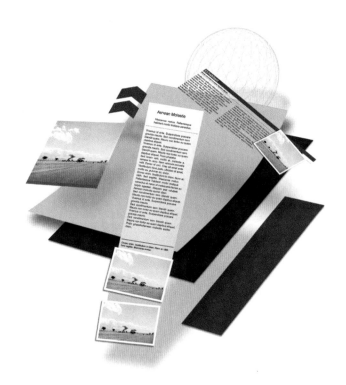

Asset Pack includes:

- 11 Graphics
- 9 Photo Frames
- 11 Page Content items

- 2 Backgrounds
- 3 Pages

Lines

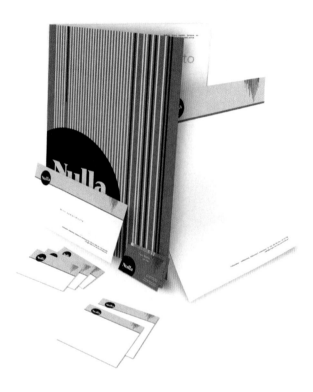

- Brochure
- Letterhead
- Compliment Slip
- Business Cards
- Address Labels

- Expense Report
- Memorandum
- Fax Transmittal
- Inventory List
- Invoice
- Time Billing
- Quotation
- Purchase Order

- Newsletter
- Envelopes
- Flyers
- Posters

Asset Pack includes:

- 9 Graphics
- 8 Photo Frames
- 15 Page Content items
- 2 Backgrounds
- 3 Pages

Renovate

- Brochure
- Letterhead
- Compliment Slip
- Business Cards
- Address Labels

- Expense Report
- Memorandum
- Fax Transmittal
- Inventory List
- Invoice
- Time Billing
- Quotation
- Purchase Order

- Newsletter
- Envelopes
- Flyers
- Posters

Asset Pack includes:

- 8 Graphics
- 7 Photo Frames
- 14 Page Content items
- 2 Backgrounds
- 3 Pages

Rugged

- Brochure
- Letterhead
- Compliment Slip
- Business Cards
- Address Labels

- Expense Report
- Memorandum
- Fax Transmittal
- Inventory List
- Invoice
- Time Billing
- Quotation
- Purchase Order

- Newsletter
- Envelopes
- Flyers
- Posters

Asset Pack includes:

- 17 Graphics
- 7 Photo Frames
- 14 Page Content items

- 2 Backgrounds
- 3 Pages

Trace

- Brochure
- Letterhead
- Compliment Slip
- Business Cards
- Address Labels

- Expense Report
- Memorandum
- Fax Transmittal
- Inventory List
- Invoice
- Time Billing
- Quotation
- Purchase Order

- Newsletter
- Envelopes
- Flyers
- Posters

Asset Pack includes:

- 24 Graphics
- 4 Photo Frames
- 29 Page Content items

- 3 Backgrounds
- 2 Pages

Bygone

- Brochure
- Letterhead
- Compliment Slip
- Business Cards
- Address Labels

- Expense Report
- Memorandum
- Fax Transmittal
- Inventory List
- Invoice
- Time Billing
- Quotation
- Purchase Order

- Newsletter
- Envelopes
- Flyers
- Posters

Asset Pack includes:

- 11 Graphics
- 6 Photo Frames
- 17 Page Content items

- 2 Backgrounds
- 3 Pages

Clouds

- Brochure
- Letterhead
- Compliment Slip
- Business Cards
- Address Labels

- Expense Report
- Memorandum
- Fax Transmittal
- Inventory List
- Invoice
- Time Billing
- Quotation
- Purchase Order

- Newsletter
- Envelopes
- Flyers
- Posters

Asset Pack includes:

- 9 Graphics
- 5 Photo Frames
- 11 Page Content items
- 2 Backgrounds
- 4 Pages

Doodle

- Brochure
- Letterhead
- Compliment Slip
- Business Cards
- Address Labels

- Expense Report
- Memorandum
- Fax Transmittal
- Inventory List
- Invoice
- Time Billing
- Quotation
- Purchase Order

- Newsletter
- Envelopes
- Flyers
- Posters

Asset Pack includes:

- 14 Graphics
- 5 Photo Frames
- 8 Page Content items
- 2 Backgrounds
- 2 Pages

Eco

- Brochure
- Letterhead
- Compliment Slip
- Business Cards
- Address Labels

- Expense Report
- Memorandum
- Fax Transmittal
- Inventory List
- Invoice
- Time Billing
- Quotation
- Purchase Order

- Newsletter
- Envelopes
- Flyers
- Posters

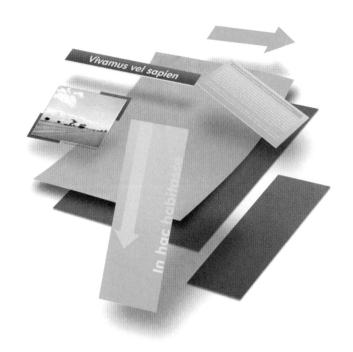

Asset Pack includes:

- 20 Graphics
- 7 Photo Frames
- 18 Page Content items
- 2 Backgrounds
- 2 Pages

Globose

- Brochure
- Letterhead
- Compliment Slip
- Business Cards
- Address Labels

- Expense Report
- Memorandum
- Fax Transmittal
- Inventory List
- Invoice
- Time Billing
- Quotation
- Purchase Order

- Newsletter
- Envelopes
- Flyers
- Posters

Asset Pack includes:

- 11 Graphics
- 5 Photo Frames
- 9 Page Content items
- 2 Backgrounds
- 3 Pages

Good Morning

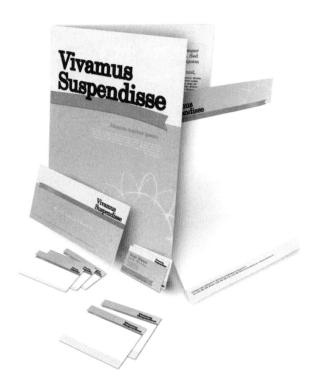

- Brochure
- Letterhead
- Compliment Slip
- Business Cards
- Address Labels

- Expense Report
- Memorandum
- Fax Transmittal
- Inventory List
- Invoice
- Time Billing
- Quotation
- Purchase Order

- Newsletter
- Envelopes
- Flyers
- Posters

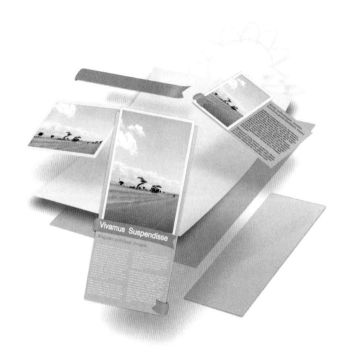

Asset Pack includes:

- 11 Graphics
- 5 Photo Frames
- 9 Page Content items
- 2 Backgrounds
- 3 Pages

Industrial

- Brochure
- Letterhead
- Compliment Slip
- Business Cards
- Address Labels

- Expense Report
- Memorandum
- Fax Transmittal
- Inventory List
- Invoice
- Time Billing
- Quotation
- Purchase Order

- Newsletter
- Envelopes
- Flyers
- Posters

Asset Pack includes:

- 14 Graphics
- 7 Photo Frames
- 20 Page Content items
- 2 Backgrounds
- 3 Pages

Ledger

- Brochure
- Letterhead
- Compliment Slip
- Business Cards
- Address Labels

- Expense Report
- Memorandum
- Fax Transmittal
- Inventory List
- Invoice
- Time Billing
- Quotation
- Purchase Order

- Newsletter
- Envelopes
- Flyers
- Posters

Asset Pack includes:

- 16 Graphics
- 6 Photo Frames
- 14 Page Content items
- 2 Backgrounds
- 3 Pages

Nature

- Brochure
- Letterhead
- Compliment Slip
- Business Cards
- Address Labels

- Expense Report
- Memorandum
- Fax Transmittal
- Inventory List
- Invoice
- Time Billing
- Quotation
- Purchase Order

- Newsletter
- Envelopes
- Flyers
- Posters

Asset Pack includes:

- 22 Graphics
- 8 Photo Frames
- 11 Page Content items
- 2 Backgrounds
- 3 Pages

Paper Office

- Brochure
- Letterhead
- Compliment Slip
- Business Cards
- Address Labels

- Expense Report
- Memorandum
- Fax Transmittal
- Inventory List
- Invoice
- Time Billing
- Quotation
- Purchase Order

- Newsletter
- Envelopes
- Flyers
- Posters

Asset Pack includes:

- 21 Graphics
- 9 Photo Frames
- 14 Page Content items
- 2 Backgrounds
- 3 Pages

Pop

- Brochure
- Letterhead
- Compliment Slip
- Business Cards
- Address Labels

- Expense Report
- Memorandum
- Fax Transmittal
- Inventory List
- Invoice
- Time Billing
- Quotation
- Purchase Order

- Newsletter
- Envelopes
- Flyers
- Posters

Asset Pack includes:

- 26 Graphics
- 12 Photo Frames
- 11 Page Content items
- 2 Backgrounds
- 2 Pages

Ribbon

- Brochure
- Letterhead
- Compliment Slip
- Business Cards
- Address Labels

- Expense Report
- Memorandum
- Fax Transmittal
- Inventory List
- Invoice
- Time Billing
- Quotation
- Purchase Order

- Newsletter
- Envelopes
- Flyers
- Posters

Asset Pack includes:

- 10 Graphics
- 7 Photo Frames
- 11 Page Content items
- 2 Backgrounds
- 3 Pages

Shabby

- Brochure
- Letterhead
- Compliment Slip
- Business Cards
- Address Labels

- Expense Report
- Memorandum
- Fax Transmittal
- Inventory List
- Invoice
- Time Billing
- Quotation
- Purchase Order

- Newsletter
- Envelopes
- Flyers
- Posters

Asset Pack includes:

- 14 Graphics
- 11 Photo Frames
- 16 Page Content items
- 2 Backgrounds
- 3 Pages

Vintage

- Brochure
- Letterhead
- Compliment Slip
- Business Cards
- Address Labels

- Expense Report
- Memorandum
- Fax Transmittal
- Inventory List
- Invoice
- Time Billing
- Quotation
- Purchase Order

- Newsletter
- Envelopes
- Flyers
- Posters

Asset Pack includes:

- 11 Graphics
- 9 Photo Frames
- 19 Page Content items
- 2 Backgrounds
- 3 Pages

Zine

- Brochure
- Letterhead
- Compliment Slip
- Business Cards
- Address Labels

- Expense Report
- Memorandum
- Fax Transmittal
- Inventory List
- Invoice
- Time Billing
- Quotation
- Purchase Order

- Newsletter
- Envelopes
- Flyers
- Posters

Asset Pack includes:

- 16 Graphics
- 6 Photo Frames
- 16 Page Content items

- 2 Backgrounds
- 2 Pages

Pro Template Packs

PagePlus provides a selection of **Pro Template Pack** templates that you can use as starting points for your own publications.

These templates provide a wide range of document types. Each themed

- Brochures
- Business Cards
- Compliment Slips
- Emails
- Envelopes
- Flyers
- Letterheads
- Logos
- Menus
- Newsletters
- Posters
- Websites

To open a Pro Template Pack template:

1   In the **Startup Wizard**, in the **Create** section, click **Use Design Template**.

2   In the dialog, click to expand the **Pro Template Packs** category and then expand the **PagePlus X6** sub-category.

3   Select a 'theme' from the list and then select the template you want to use in the centre pane.

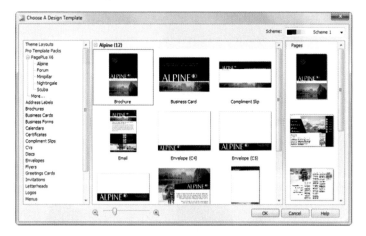

 For more information about **Design Templates**, see *Creating a publication from design templates* in PagePlus Help.

4   Click **OK** to open selected the template.

The following pages provide previews of the **Pro Template Packs** templates provided with **PagePlus X6**.

 You can also get more **Pro Template Packs** from the template store. Visit http://www.serif.com/templates

Alpine

- Brochure
- Business Card
- Compliment Slip
- Letterhead

- Envelopes
- Flyer
- Logo
- Newsletter
- Poster

- Email
- Website

Forum

- Brochure
- Business Card
- Compliment Slip
- Letterhead

- Envelopes
- Flyer
- Logo
- Newsletter
- Poster

- Email
- Website

Minipillar

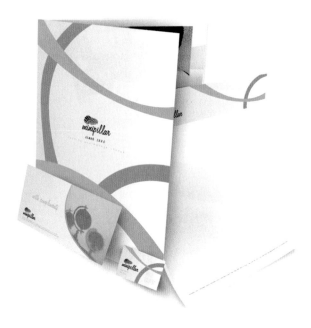

- Brochure
- Business Card
- Compliment Slip
- Letterhead

- Envelopes
- Flyer
- Logo
- Newsletter
- Poster

- Email
- Website

Nightingale

- Brochure
- Business Card
- Compliment Slip
- Letterhead

- Envelopes
- Flyer
- Logo
- Newsletter
- Poster

- Email
- Website

Scuba

- Brochure
- Business Card
- Compliment Slip
- Letterhead

- Envelopes
- Flyer
- Logo
- Newsletter
- Poster

- Email

- Website